A THEORY OF WORD ORDER
WITH SPECIAL REFERENCE
TO SPANISH

NORTH-HOLLAND   29
LINGUISTIC SERIES
Edited by S.C. DIK and J.G. KOOIJ

A THEORY OF WORD ORDER WITH SPECIAL REFERENCE TO SPANISH

Heles Contreras

University of Washington, Seattle

1976

NORTH-HOLLAND PUBLISHING COMPANY
AMSTERDAM · NEW YORK · OXFORD

© NORTH-HOLLAND PUBLISHING COMPANY - 1976

ISBN North-Holland: 07204 6210 x
ISBN American Elsevier: 0444 11119 0

Published by:
NORTH-HOLLAND PUBLISHING COMPANY
AMSTERDAM • NEW YORK • OXFORD

Sole distributors for the U.S.A. and Canada:

AMERICAN ELSEVIER PUBLISHING COMPANY, INC.
52 VANDERBILT AVENUE
NEW YORK, N.Y. 10017

Library of Congress Cataloging in Publication Data

Contreras, Heles.
   A theory of word order with special reference to
Spanish.

   (North-Holland linguistic series ; 29)
   Bibliography: p.
   Includes indexes.
   1. Grammar, Comparative and general--Word order.
2. Spanish language--Word order.   I.   Title.
P295.C63   415   76-10157
ISBN 0-7204-6210-X

PRINTED IN THE NETHERLANDS

To

Patricio
Moyra
Sandra
Carmen
Leticia

an unordered,
on occasion disorderly,
set.

PREFACE

I have long admired Dwight Bolinger for the subtlety of
his linguistic insights. It was the reading of his work on
word order and sentential stress that first got me interested
in this topic and led me to a re-examination of the work of
Mathesius and his followers, as well as to the discovery of the
priceless research of Anna Granville Hatcher.

The long process that started with the critical reading of
various articles and books on word order, primarily from the
viewpoint of the functional sentence perspective, and culmina-
ted with the present study, quite tentative to be sure, was
made possible by a combination of factors, two of which I would
like to single out. First, the support of my students at the
University of Washington, who in a couple of seminars helped
me, sometimes unwittingly, to refine what at first were gross
attempts at generalizations; second, a sabbatical leave gran-
ted by the University of Washington, which gave me the time to
complete this study.

To both my students and the University of Washington I
hereby express my gratitude.

Finally, lest my criticism of the transformational approach
to word order be misunderstood, I must make the rather obvious
statement that, had it not been for my exposure to and great
admiration for Chomsky and his followers, this study would never have achieved the level of explicitness which it has.

                                        Heles Contreras

TABLE OF CONTENTS

x

INTRODUCTION

The treatment of word order has so far been highly unsatisfactory. On the one hand, there is a Prague-school tradition going back to Mathesius which, although rich in insights concerning the informational content of the sentence and its importance for word order and other phenomena, has always remained highly speculative and fairly inexplicit. On the other, transformational grammar, which has only recently recognized the importance of given and new information (under the misleading labels of presupposition and focus), has either relegated most of the relevant phenomena to the limbo of 'stylistic reordering', presumably in the domain of linguistic performance, or failed to go beyond the most elementary attempts at the formulation of word order rules.

Given this lack of any semblance of theory of word order, it is hardly surprising that no serious treatment of the subject as it concerns Spanish is to be found. Linguists like Bolinger and Hatcher have contributed, to be sure, a number of significant observations concerning word order in Spanish, but they have failed to develop them into an explicit set of rules.

This study is an attempt to fill both the general and the specifically Spanish lacunae.

The vastness of the subject which this study deals with imposes some limitations of scope. We consider only the relative order of major sentence constituents, not their internal structure. Nothing is said here, consequently, about the interesting problem of the internal order of noun phrases. The reader is referred to Bolinger (1954-5) and Stiehm (1975) for insightful observations concerning this topic.

We also exclude questions, exclamations and commands, and concentrate exclusively on declarative sentences. In doing so, we are no doubt neglecting some important data. It would seem, however, that the rules presented throughout this study could be easily extended to non-declarative sentences. Thus, in the case of the following Venezuelan road sign,

(0.1) Estacione en el hombrillo.
'Park on the shoulder.'

a theme/rheme analysis proves quite illuminating.

A literal-minded policeman could conceivably operate under the assumption that the regulation referred to by the sign may be violated not only by parking on the circulating lanes but also by failing to stop and park on the shoulder when the sign is sighted. In terms of a theme/rheme analysis, sentence (0.1) is in fact ambiguous: either the whole sentence is a rheme (='new' information; this is the improbable interpretation), or estacione 'park' is the theme (='given' information) and en el hombrillo 'on the shoulder' the rheme, that is, the sign is interpreted as meaning 'if you park, do it on the shoulder.'

In the course of our study, we identify certain elements as rheme-markers, or 'rhematizers'. This notion is quite pertinent to the interpretation of (0.1), since its ambiguity disappears if we insert a rhematizer like sólo 'only' in front of en el hombrillo 'on the shoulder.' Our literal-minded policeman could no longer give you a citation for failing to stop and park when you see the sign, if it were modified to read as in (0.2).

(0.2) Estacione sólo en el hombrillo.
      'Park only on the shoulder.'

It is clear, then, that a theme/rheme analysis is quite appropriate
for non-declarative sentences, but it would probably take another book to
examine the specific problems of such sentences.

Beginning with a demonstration of the crucial role of given (theme)
and new (rheme) information in the grammar of Spanish, this study progres-
ses towards the formulation of a number of explicit rules which generate a
variety of surface orders, adequately pairing them up with the appropriate
underlying structures.

In contrast with other treatments of word order, this study recognizes
the interrelationship of linear order and prosodic phenomena, and formul-
ates rules to account for it.

Independent factors, such as the internal complexity of sentence constituents, are shown to play a role in determining linear order, and to be
related in nontrivial ways to the main determining factor thereof, namely
what is here called the rhematic structure of the sentence.

Finally, it is shown that the analysis proposed here has significant
implications for the definition of 'functional' syntactic notions like
subject and object as well as for the analysis of sentences with indeterminate subjects.

Chapter One

GIVEN AND NEW INFORMATION

1.1.1 Introduction

Linguistic communication may be characterized in the following terms:
the speaker attempts to bring to the addressee's consciousness certain
communicative units which (s)he assumes not to be there at the moment of
communication. In this attempt, the speaker may or may not mention other
units which (s)he assumes <u>are</u> present in the addressee's consciousness.[1]

Thus, if María happens to run into Pedro when he is about to bite
into a nice apple, she may say:

(1.1) ¡Qué LINDA la manzana![2]
'What a NICE apple!'

or just:

(1.2) ¡Qué LINDA!
'How NICE!'

When uttering (1.1), María is signaling through the placement of
the main sentential stress that the 'new' communicative unit she wants
to bring to Pedro's consciousness is ¡qué linda!, and that she assumes
the concept <u>manzana</u> to be already present there. Since the communicative
context lends plausibility to such an assumption, María may limit her-
self to the utterance of (1.2), which contains only those elements which
may be considered 'new'.

This simple example shows that the placement of sentential stress
plays an essential role in distinguishing 'given' from 'new' information.
Another important factor is word order. Let us assume that after her initial statement María wants to talk to Pedro about her activities of the
day, and says:

(1.3) El experimento FRACASÓ.
'The experiment FAILED.'

Since there is no reason to assume that the notion <u>experimento</u> is
in Pedro's consciousness at the moment, the whole sentence must be taken
as new information. However, the same sentence would also be appropriate
in a situation where <u>experimento</u> had already been introduced, for instance, as an answer to Pedro's question:

(1.4) ¿Cómo resultó el experimento?
'How did the experiment turn out?'

On the other hand, it would be inappropriate for María to utter
sentence (1.5),

(1.5) FRACASÓ el experimento.
'The experiment FAILED.'

unless she had just been asked a question like (1.4) or there was some
other indication that the notion <u>experimento</u> was in Pedro's consciousness at that moment.

This example shows that whereas elements preceding the main sentential stress may or may not be interpreted as new information, those
that follow it must necessarily be interpreted as information already

present in the addressee's consciousness.
      The dichotomy given/new information is relevant not only to senten-
tial stress and word order but also to the processes of deletion and pronominalization as well as to other grammatical features, such as the
choice between a definite and an indefinite article. Let us illustrate
the latter first. If María, instead of uttering sentence (1.3) says

> (1.6) Un experimento FRACASÓ.
>   'An experiment FAILED.'

the whole sentence must necessarily be taken as new information, thus
contrasting with (1.3), where the definite noun phrase may either be
given or new information. This propensity of indefinite noun phrases to
function as new information explains the anomaly of a string like the
following,

> (1.7) *FRACASÓ un experimento.
>   'An experiment FAILED.'

since a clash is produced between, on the one hand, the principle that
post-stress elements are to be interpreted as given information, and, on
the other, the requirement that indefinite noun phrases be interpreted
as new information.
      Let us now illustrate the relationship between the given/new inform-
ation dichotomy and the processes of deletion and pronominalization.
Let us assume that Pedro asks María:

> (1.4) ¿Cómo resultó el experimento?
>   'How did the experiment turn out?'

Besides answers (1.3) and (1.5), the following are also permissible:

> (1.8) FRACASÓ.
>   'It FAILED.'

> (1.9) No lo HICE.
>   'I didn't DO it.'

In other words, it possible to delete or pronominalize the noun
phrase el experimento, which contains given information. On the other
hand, since in these examples the verb is obligatorily interpreted as
new information, neither its deletion nor its replacement by an anaphoric expression are permissible.
      It should not surprise us, in view of these examples, that the
transformational attempts to account for deletion[3] and pronominalization,[4]
which do not take into account the distinction between given and new information, have so far proved to be inadequate.

1.1.2 Given/new versus presupposition/focus

Since the terms presupposition and focus suggested, among others,
by Chomsky (1969:18) and Jackendoff (1972:229) seem to refer to the same
notions that we have been labelling as given and new information, our
terminological preference should be justified.
      Let us consider one of Chomsky's examples:

> (1.10) Is it JOHN who writes poetry?

In this sentence, John is identified as the focus, the presupposition being 'X writes poetry'. This allows Chomsky to explain that while
(1.11) is an acceptable answer to (1.10),

(1.11) No, it is BILL who writes poetry.

because it contains the same presupposition, sentence (1.12) is not,

(1.12) No, John writes only short STORIES.

since its presupposition does not match that of the question.

It is clear that the distinction Chomsky tries to capture with the terms presupposition and focus is identical to the one we have been dealing with under the terms given and new. Chomsky's use of presupposition, however, conflicts with another concept firmly established in the literature. The following example will illustrate this statement. Suppose that Pedrito comes home after his first day of school, and when asked by his mother,

(1.13) ¿Qué aprendiste hoy, Pedrito?
       'What did you learn today, Pedrito?'

replies:

(1.14) Aprendí que dos y dos son cuatro.
       'I learned that two and two is four.'

Following Chomsky's analysis, we must say that the presupposition shared by the question and the answer is 'Pedrito learned X', and that the focus of the answer is the clause 'that two and two is four'. The trouble with the use of the terms presupposition and focus in this way is that it conflicts with the widely accepted notion of presupposition as 'assumed by the speaker to be true',[5] according to which the clause 'that two and two is four' is presupposed, since it is in the nature of the verb to learn, as opposed to a verb like to believe, that its complement is assumed by the speaker to refer to a true fact.

We are faced, then, with the confusing situation that the focus, which of course may not be 'presupposed' by Chomsky's definition, may or may not be 'presupposed' by most other linguists' definition. Thus, in (1.14) the focus que dos y dos son cuatro 'that two and two is four' is presupposed (to be true), but in (1.15) it is not.

(1.15) No aprendí nada, pero el profesor dice que dos y dos son
       cuatro.
       'I didn't learn anything, but the teacher says that two
       and two is four.'

By uttering (1.15), precocious Pedrito signals his refusal to believe what the teacher has told him, which is not the case if he utters (1.14). In both cases, however, the clause que dos y dos son cuatro 'that two and two is four' contains new information.

A real example of the confusion created by Chomsky's use of presupposition is the following criticism by Lakoff (1969:29):

'Of course, the Halliday-Chomsky account of focus is not quite correct. For example, Halliday and Chomsky assume that the constituent bearing main stress in the surface structure is the focus, and therefore that the lexical items in that constituent provide new rather than presupposed information. This is not in general the case. Consider (37).

(37) The TALL girl left.

Here the main stress is on TALL, which should be the focus according to Halliday and Chomsky, and should therefore

be new, not given, information. However, in (37), TALL
is understood as modifying the noun in the same way as
the restrictive relative clause who was tall. Since restrictive relative clauses are presupposed, it follows
that in (37), it is presupposed, not asserted, that the
girl being spoken of was tall.'

It should be clear that the fallacy in Lakoff's argument stems from
his use of the term presupposition with two different meanings. If we
distinguish between a-presupposition (the assumption that X is true) and
b-presupposition (the assumption that X is present in the addressee's
consciousness), Lakoff's statement amounts to saying that since the adjective tall is a-presupposed, it must necessarily be b-presupposed. The
logic is, of course, faulty, but at least part of the blame must rest
with Chomsky for using the term presupposition in an unconventional way
without warning.

In view of these considerations, it seems clearly advisable to avoid
the use of the terms presupposition and focus in the sense of 'given' and
'new' information.

1.1.3 Given/new versus theme/rheme

It is also necessary to compare the terms given and new with the
Prague school terminology.[6] On the basis of the concept of communicative
dynamism, defined as the relative contribution of an element to the communication, Firbas (1966) distinguishes theme, transition and rheme, as
placed on an ascending scale.

As Chafe (1974) has perceptively pointed out, it is not easy to fit
the term transition within our framework: either the speaker assumes an
element to be present in the addressee's consciousness or (s)he does not;
it makes no sense to talk about elements which are half present.

However, if we disregard the term transition, the remaining terms
theme and rheme are quite convenient to designate the notions 'given' and
'new', and present the advantage of derivational productivity: an element
may be referred to as thematic or rhematic, it is possible thematize or
rhematize a constituent, some elements may be said to function as rhematizers, etc.

We will, consequently, use the terms theme and rheme and their der-
ivatives interchangeably with the terms given and new, but will ask the
reader to keep in mind that our definition of these terms is not identical to that of the Prague school.

1.2 The grammatical relevance of given and new information

1.2.1 Introduction

The stress placement and word order phenomena briefly illustrated at
the beginning of this chapter are often considered to fall under the domain of stylistics.[7] In the remainder of this chapter, this position will
be shown to be in error, since the phenomena we are concerned with are
not only central to the semantic interpretation of the sentence but also
play a crucial role in the operation of certain syntactic transformations,
particularly those involving deletion and pronominalization.

If by stylistic phenomenon we understand the variation resulting
from free choices made by the speaker, it is clear that the location of
the main sentential stress and the linear distribution of most syntactic
constituents are not stylistic phenomena.

Thus, for instance, a speaker of Spanish would normally not initiate a discourse with sentences like (1.16) or (1.17).

(1.16) La resistencia EMPEZÓ.
'The resistance STARTED.'

(1.17) La RESISTENCIA empezó.
'The RESISTANCE started.'

For (1.16) to be adequate the speaker must have reason to assume that the concept of 'resistance' is in the addressee's consciousness, and that assumption would normally be unwarranted if nothing had been said previously.

Similarly, for (1.17) to be adequate, the speaker must assume that the concept of 'starting' is present in the addressee's consciousness. On the other hand, a sentence like (1.18)

(1.18) Empezó la RESISTENCIA.
'The RESISTANCE started.'

is perfectly adequate in discourse-initial position, as well as in answer to a question like (1.19).

(1.19) ¿Qué empezó?
'What started?'

The speaker does not have entire freedom, then, in selecting a certain word order or in assigning sentential stress.

Correspondingly, the hearer is severely constricted by word order and sentential stress location as to the inferences (s)he can make. To the extent that these inferences match what is actually present in or absent from the hearer's consciousness, the message is perceived as adequate.

This would seem to suggest that the task of reducing sentential stress and word order phenomena to an explicit theory is practically impossible, since it requires access to the consciousness of the interlocutors as well as information about the extralinguistic contingencies that may condition these phenomena. Fortunately, this is not the case. It is possible, as we will try to show throughout this study, to formulate a theory of word order and stress placement that will predict what inferences are allowed given a certain stress placement and a certain word order with respect to what the speaker assumes to be present in or absent from the addressee's consciousness, without having access to the speaker's or the hearer's mind, and without including extralinguistic factors in the theory.

1.2.2 Semantic relevance of given and new information

We have shown that the placement of sentential stress and the choice of word order do not result from free choices made by the speaker.

Let us now consider briefly the semantic import of sentential stress placement and word order. If we consider, for instance, the fact that whereas sentences like those in (1.20) are perfectly grammatical,

(1.20) a. Espero que triunfe la RESISTENCIA, no la DICTADURA.
'I hope the RESISTANCE will win, not the DICTATORSHIP.'

b. Espero que la resistencia TRIUNFE, no que FRACASE.
'I hope the resistance WINS, not that it FAILS.'

those in (1.21) are not,

(1.21) a. *Espero que triunfe la RESISTENCIA, no que FRACASE.
          'I hope the RESISTANCE wins, not that it FAILS.'

       b. *Espero que la resistencia TRIUNFE, no la DICTADURA.
          'I hope the resistance WINS, not the DICTATORSHIP.'

it should be clear that sentential stress placement and word order con-
tribute to the determination of semantic well-formedness in a rather
crucial way. The difference between the well-formed sentences in (1.20)
and the anomalous sentences in (1.21) is clearly not a matter of stylistic preference.
    Another example of the semantic relevance of word order and senten-
tial stress placement is the following. An adverbial expression like por
supuesto 'of course' may combine freely with any sentence, regardless of
order and stress location. Thus, for instance, both (1.22) and (1.23) are
grammatical.

(1.22) Por supuesto, la resistencia TRIUNFARÁ.
       'Of course, the resistance will WIN.'

(1.23) Por supuesto, triunfará la RESISTENCIA.
       'Of course, the RESISTANCE will win.'

On the other hand, an adverb like astutamente 'cleverly' combines
only with sentences of type (1.22), where the agent does not carry the
main sentential stress. Thus, (1.24) is grammatical, but not (1.25).

(1.24) Astutamente, la resistencia se REPLEGÓ.
       'Cleverly, the resistance RETREATED.'

(1.25) *Astutamente, se replegó la RESISTENCIA.
       'Cleverly, the RESISTANCE retreated.'

    Besides confirming the general relevance of word order and senten-
tial stress placement for semantic interpretation, this example suggests
that Chomsky's (1969) view that given and new information are determined
in surface structure is incompatible with his view that lexical insertion
takes place in deep structure: if the deep structure contains no information as to what is 'given' and what is 'new', the grammar cannot decide
when it is permissible to insert lexical items of the class of astutamente 'cleverly'.[8]

1.2.3 Syntactic relevance of given and new information

    We will now examine some syntactic transformations which depend on
the distribution of given and new information, henceforth, the rhematic
structure of the sentence.
    Our first example is the rule of CONJUNCTION, formulated by Chomsky
(1957:36) in the following way:

(1.26) If S_1 and S_2 are grammatical sentences, and S_1
       differs from S_2 only in that X appears in S_1
       where Y appears in S_2 (i.e., S_1 = ..X.. and
       S_2 = ..Y..), and X and Y are constituents of
       the same type in S_1 and S_2, respectively, then
       S_3 is a sentence, where S_3 is the result of
       replacing X by X+and+Y in S_1 (i.e., S_3 =
       ..X+and+Y..).

Let us assume that S_1 and S_2 are (1.27) and (1.28) respectively.

(1.27) Algún día el pueblo TRIUNFARÁ.
'Some day the people will WIN.'

(1.28) Algún día la resistencia TRIUNFARÁ.
'Some day the resistance will WIN.'

In terms of Chomsky's formulation, X is el pueblo, and Y la resistencia, and it is possible to form a sentence S_3 identical to S_1, but with el pueblo y la resistencia instead of el pueblo, since presumably el pueblo and la resistencia are 'constituents of the same type.' Applying this rule plus the rule of subject-verb agreement, we obtain the following sentence:

(1.29) Algún día el pueblo y la resistencia TRIUNFARÁN.
'Some day the people and the resistance will WIN.'

Notice, however, that in order for the rule of CONJUNCTION to apply correctly, the phrase 'constituents of the same type', which Chomsky does not define, must be interpreted as including not only syntactic similarity -- X cannot be a noun phrase if Y is a verb -- but also rhematic function. Thus, if X is theme and Y rheme, even though both are noun phrases, the rule does not appIly. Thus, if S_1 is (1.30),

(1.30) Algún día triunfará el PUEBLO.
'Some day the PEOPLE will win.'

its conjunction with S_2 (1.28) produces not (1.29) but a sentence like the following:

(1.31) Algún día la resistencia TRIUNFARÁ, y triunfará el PUEBLO.
'Some day the resistance will WIN, and the PEOPLE will win.'

In fact, the rhematic structure of the sentence seems to override even syntactic function (i.e. subject, object, etc.) for the purposes of this rule. Thus, on the basis of an S_1 like (1.32) and an S_2 like (1.33),

(1.32) Las virtudes no NACEN.
'Virtues are not BORN.'

(1.33) Las virtudes se HACEN.
'Virtues are MADE.'

it is possible to form an S_3 like (1.34),

(1.34) Las virtudes no NACEN, se HACEN.
'Virtues are not BORN, they are MADE.'

in spite of the fact that las virtudes is subject in S_1 and direct object in S_2. Quite clearly, the rule of CONJUNCTION is applicable in this case because the rhematic structure of the conjuncts is parallel. If S_2 had las virtudes as rheme, it could not combine with S_1 to produce S_3.

Just in case the reader is wondering whether our analysis of las virtudes as direct object in (1.33) is adequate, in view of the fact that the verb agrees with it, let us look at the following variant of (1.34) where las virtudes cannot possibly be interpreted as subject:[9]

(1.35) Las virtudes no NACEN, se las HACE.
'Virtues are not BORN, they are MADE.'

Given this example, there can be no possible doubt that 'constituents of the same type' may have a different syntactic function provided they are comparable in rhematic terms.

Another syntactic transformation which requires information about

the rhematic structure of the sentence is GAPPING, a rule which converts
(1.36) into (1.37).

(1.36) Perú nacionalizó el PETRÓLEO, y Venezuela nacionalizó el
       HIERRO.
       'Perú nationalized OIL, and Venezuela nationalized IRON.'

(1.37) Perú nacionalizó el PETRÓLEO, y Venezuela el HIERRO.
       'Perú nationalized OIL, and Venezuela IRON.'

The deletion of the verb repeated in the second conjunct is possible
because both conjuncts have a parallel rhematic structure; otherwise, the
rule would not apply. Thus, sentence (1.38) cannot undergo GAPPING,

(1.38) Algunos gorilas ODIAN a los intelectuales, y algunos gorilas
       odian al PUEBLO.
       'Some gorillas HATE intellectuals, and some gorillas hate the
       PEOPLE.'

since the rhematic structure of its conjuncts is not parallel:

(1.39) *Algunos gorilas ODIAN a los intelectuales, y algunos (gori-
       las) al PUEBLO.
       'Some gorillas HATE intellectuals, and some (gorillas) the
       PEOPLE.'

It is not surprising, given these facts, that previous attempts to
account for the operation of GAPPING which disregard rhematic structure
fail to account for the data. This is the case of Hankamer (1973), for
instance. He claims that a sentence like (1.40) is not ambiguous,

(1.40) Jack wants Mike to wash himself and Arnie to shave himself.

since it can only be interpreted as a reduced version of (1.41), not of
(1.42).

(1.41) Jack wants Mike to wash himself, and Jack wants Arnie to
       shave himself.

(1.42) Jack wants Mike to wash himself, and Arnie wants Mike to
       shave himself.

Since an unrestricted application of GAPPING would derive (1.40)
from both of these underlying structures, Hankamer proposes the following principle to explain the alleged non-ambiguity of this sentense:

(1.43) Any application of GAPPING which would yield an output
       structure identical to a structure derivable by GAPPING
       from another source, but with the "gap" at the left ex-
       tremity, is disallowed (p. 29).

This principle would account for the facts as presented by Hankamer.
However, these facts are more complex than Hankamer would lead us to believe. Thus, the readings disallowed by Hankamer's principle are quite
acceptable with the right kind of intonation and stress pattern. For
instance, (1.44), pronounced with a pause after _Arnie_,

(1.44) JACK wants Mike to WASH himself, and ARNIE // to SHAVE
       himself.

has precisely the interpretation which Hankamer's principle rules out,
namely, (1.45).

(1.45) Jack wants Mike to wash himself, and Arnie wants Mike to shave himself.

If, on the other hand, our formulation of GAPPING takes into account the rhematic structure of the sentence, as in (1.46), there is no problem.

(1.46) An element can be 'gapped' only if the element to which it bears identity has the feature [-rheme].[10]

Since in the first conjunct of (1.41), Jack wants is not a rheme, its second occurrence, in the second conjunct, may be deleted; this gives us the interpretation allowed by Hankamer. Similarly, since in (1.42) wants Mike may be interprted as non-rhematic, its deletion in the second conjunct is permissible; this gives us the interpretation disallowed by Hankamer, namely (1.44).

Our formulation also accounts for cases like (1.47),

(1.47) Jack likes Sally more than Susan.

which Hankamer himself presents as a counterexample to his principle.

According to Hankamer's 'no-ambiguity condition', this sentence should be interpreted only as (1.48), not as (1.49).

(1.48) Jack likes Sally more than Jack likes Susan.

(1.49) Jack likes Sally more than Susan likes Sally.

In fact, given the appropriate stress and intonational patter, (1.47) may be interpreted either as (1.48) or as (1.49). In the following version

(1.50) Jack likes SALLY more than SUSAN.

the meaning is that of (1.48), whereas in version (1.51),

(1.51) JACK likes Sally more than SUSAN.

the meaning is that of (1.49). These are precisely the interpretations which our principle predicts. Thus, given a structure like (1.52),

(1.52) Jack likes SALLY more than Jack likes SUSAN.

it is possible to delete the phrase Jack likes in the second clause because of its non-rhematic character in the first; we thus obtain sentence (1.50).

Similarly, given a structure like (1.53),

(1.53) JACK likes Sally more than SUSAN likes Sally.

the deletion of likes Sally in the second clause is possible because of the non-rhematic character of the identical phrase in the first clause.

Finally, our condition on GAPPING, coupled with a special assumption about the rhematic properties of negation, explains the facts, pointed out by Jackendoff (1971:27), pertaining to string (1.54),

(1.54) *Bill didn't eat the peaches, nor Harry.

whose ungrammaticality seems difficult to explain given the well-formedness of the corresponding affirmative sentence:

(1.55) Either Bill ate the peaches, or Harry.

In fact, the ungrammaticality of (1.54) is simply due to the use of nor without its correlative neither, as shown by the fact that (1.56) is perfectly grammatical,

(1.56) Neither BILL ate the peaches, nor HARRY.

as well as by the fact that (1.55) becomes ungrammatical if we use only
the second of the two correlative conjunctions:

(1.57) *BILL ate the peaches, or HARRY.

All other facts related to these sentences are explainable in terms
of rhematic structure.

As we will see in chapter six, the presence of negation normally
forces a rhematic interpretation of the constituent being negated. In
(1.54), the negation may affect different constituents, and that determines which elements of the second conjunct may be deleted. If the whole
sentence is within the scope of the negation, as in (1.58),

(1.58) Bill didn't eat the peaches, Harry didn't make the salad; no-
      body did what they were supposed to do.

in which case the intonation of the first conjunct is sustained at a mid
level pitch, no deletion is possible; thus all of the following sentences
are ungrammatical:

(1.59) a. *Bill didn't eat the peaches⃗ ; HARRY did.
      b. *Bill didn't eat the peaches⃗ ; (he ate) the SALAD.
      c. *Bill didn't eat the peaches ; he made the SALAD.

If, on the other hand, only the direct object is within the scope of
the negation, as in (1.60),

(1.60) Bill didn't eat the PEACHES.

all or part of the non-negated portion of the sentence may be deleted
(or pronominalized) in the second conjunct, as shown in (1.61),

(1.61) a. Bill didn't eat the PEACHES, he ate the SALAD.
      b. Bill didn't eat the PEACHES, but the SALAD.

but the negated element cannot be deleted:

(1.62) *Bill didn't eat the PEACHES, HARRY did.

Similarly, if the whole verb phrase is within the scope of the negation, in which case the surface representation is identical to (1.60),
only the non-negated element, i.e. the subject, may be pronominalized:

(1.63) Bill didn't eat the PEACHES, he made the SALAD.

Finally, if the negation affects only the subject, as in (1.64) or
(1.65),

(1.64) BILL didn't eat the peaches.

(1.65) Neither BILL ate the peaches...

it is possible to delete or pronominalize other elements:

(1.66) a. BILL didn't eat the peaches, HARRY did.
      b. Neither BILL ate the peaches, nor HARRY.

So far, we have seen that theme and rheme are relavnt to the rules
of CONJUNCTION and GAPPING. I will now present some evidence pointing to
the relevance of these notions to the applicability of a rule which Hooper
and Thompson (1973) have called COMPLEMENT PREPOSING, and which is illustrated by (1.67),

(1.67) It's just started to rain, he said.

where the complement of <u>said</u> has been moved to the front of the sentence
from its underlying post-verbal position.

Hooper and Thompson note the ungrammaticality of a sentence similar
to (1.67) but with a negated main clause:

(1.68) * It's started to rain, he didn't say.

Within a theme/rheme framework, the difference in grammaticality
between (1.67) and (1.68) can be accounted for by restricting COMPLEMENT
PREPOSING to rhematic complements and by assuming that negated constituents rank high in the rheme selection hierarchy.[11] This means than in
its most common interpretation, (1.68) will have the phrase <u>he didn't say</u>
as rheme and the complement as theme. Given our formulation of COMPLEMENT
PREPOSING, the rule does not apply to the underlying structure of (1.68),
whereas in (1.67), where the complement must be interpreted as rhematic,
its preposing is allowed.

This explanation is also valid for Spanish cases of COMPLEMENT PRE-
POSING. Consider, for example, the following sentences:

(1.69) a. Creo que va a LLOVER.
          'I think it's going to RAIN.'

       b. Va a LLOVER, creo.
          'It's going to RAIN, I think.'

(1.70) a. No CREO que vaya a llover.
          'I DON'T think it's going to rain.'

       b. *Va(ya) a llover, no CREO.
          'It's going to rain, I DON'T think.'

The rhematic complement in (1.69) can be preposed, but not so the
complement in (1.70), which is thematic. That this is really the important difference between (1.69) and (1.70), and not merely the presence or
absence of a negation in the main clause, can be shown by changing the
theme/rheme distribution of (1.70) to that of (1.71).

(1.71) No creo que vaya a LLOVER.
       (In answer to ¿Qué es lo que no crees? 'What is it you
       don't believe?').

We observe that the complement is now eligible for preposing, since
it is rhematic:

(1.72) Que va(ya) a LLOVER no creo.
       'That it's going to RAIN I don't believe."

Another indication that the relevant difference between (1.69) and
(1.70) is the theme/rheme arrangement, and not the presence or absence
of a negation, is found in sentences where the rhematic function is as-
sociated with elements other than the negation, for instance the adverb
<u>sólo</u> 'only':

(1.73) Sólo SOSPECHO que va a llover (no tengo certeza).
       'I only SUSPECT it's going to rain (I'm not certain).'

Predictably, according to our analysis, the complement cannot be
preposed since it is not rhematic:

(1.74) *Va a llover, sólo SOSPECHO.
       'It's going to rain, I only SUSPECT.'

It is not the case, as might be argued, that verbs like <u>sospechar</u>
'to suspect' block COMPLEMENT PREPOSING, as shown by (1.75):

(1.75) a. Sospecho que va a LLOVER.
          'I suspect it's going to RAIN.'

      b. Va a LLOVER, sospecho.
          'It's going to RAIN, I suspect.'

As a final piece of evidence for the crucial role of theme and rheme
in the operation of syntactic rules, consider Emonds' (1969) Root Transformations, which, as Hooper and Thompson (1973) have shown, apply only
to assertive sentences, both embedded and non-embedded. This is illustrated by the following examples:

(1.76) Never have I seen such a mess.

(1.77) I insist that never have I seen such a mess.

(1.78) *I am happy that never have I seen such a mess.

where NEGATIVE CONSTITUENT PREPOSING, a root transformation, produces
grammatical sentences in (1.76) and (1.77) since the clause containing
the negation is an assertion, but when applied to the non-assertive complement of (1.78) produces an ungrammatical string.[12]

Many of these root transformations which produce 'emphatic' sentences
in English do not have that effect in Spanish, as Terrell (forthcoming)
has shown. Consider, for instance, the following sentences:

(1.79) Over the trees flew many birds.

(1.80) He said that over the trees flew many birds.

(1.81) *I'm happy that over the trees flew many birds.

which illustrate the applicability of DIRECTIONAL ADVERB PREPOSING to the
assertive clauses of (1.79) and (1.80), and its non-applicability to the
non-assertive complement of (1.81). In Spanish, however, all of the following, which correspond directly to (1.79) - (1.81), are grammatical:

(1.82) Sobre los árboles volaban muchos pájaros.

(1.83) Dijo que sobre los árboles volaban muchos pájaros.

(1.84) Me alegro de que sobre los árboles volaran muchos pájaros.

If the condition on the applicability of root transformations suggested by Hooper and Thompson is valid, DIRECTIONAL ADVERB PREPOSING is
not a root transformation in Spanish, although it is in English, as shown
by the fact that preposed directional adverbs are possible in assertive
clauses such as (1.82) and (1.83) as well as in non-assertive clauses
like the one in (1.84). In fact, as suggested by Terrell (forthcoming)
and supported by further evidence in this study, the rule of DIRECTIONAL
ADVERB PREPOSING does not even exist in Spanish.

If we try to answer the question of what constitutes a root transformation in Spanish, we see again the need to appeal to the notions of
theme and rheme. Notice that in the sentences (1.82) - (1.84), the rheme
is in final position. If we consider this the normal, non-emphatic, order,
a root transformation may be defined as one that alters it, that is, that
preposes the rheme.

Compare, for example, sentence (1.85),

(1.85) Mañana lo OPERAN.
          'Tomorrow they OPERATE on him.'

with a 'normal' order theme + rheme, to sentence (1.86),

(1.86) MAÑANA lo operan.
'They operate on him TOMORROW.'

with an 'inverted' order rheme + theme.
Our definition of root transformation, together with Hooper and
Thompson's condition on the applicability of root transformations, predict
that (1.85) will occur both as an assertive and as a non-assertive clause,
whereas (1.86) will occur only as an assertive clause. The following sentences show that in fact this prediction is borne out:

(1.87) a. Dice que mañana lo OPERAN.
'He says that tomorrow they OPERATE on him.'

b. Siento que mañana lo OPEREN.
'I'm sorry that they OPERATE on him tomorrow.'

(1.88) a. Dice que MAÑANA lo operan.
'He says that TOMORROW they operate on him.'

b. *Siento que MAÑANA lo operen.
'I'm sorry that TOMORROW they operate on him.'

Notice, furthermore, that the only way to relate the oddity of
(1.88b) to that of (1.89)

(1.89) *Siento que JUAN venga.
'I'm sorry that JOHN is coming.'
(Cf. Siento que venga JUAN.
'I'm sorry that JOHN is coming.'
Siento que Juan VENGA.
'I'm sorry that John is COMING.')

is by defining Spanish root transformations in terms of theme and rheme,
since only this makes it possible to say that (1.89) has in fact undergone a transformation, namely the optional transformation that changes
the normal word order theme + rheme into the marked order rheme + theme.
If Spanish root transformations are defined in terms of categories like
subject and object, the complement of (1.89) must of course be considered
to occur in the normal unmarked order, and the oddity of the sentence explained independently from that of (1.88b). The unified explanation made
possible by our definition of root transformation is a strong argument in
its favor.

1.3 Conclusion

In conclusion, there seems to be abundant evidence that the notions
of theme and rheme occupy a central position in the structure of Spanish
sentences, since they determine not only semantic interpretation but also
the operation of certain syntactic transformations, especially those involving deletion and movement.

FOOTNOTES TO CHAPTER ONE

1
This chapter owes much to Chafe 1974.

2
Capitals signal the location of the main sentential stress.

3
See, for instance, Hankamer 1973, Jackendoff 1971, Koutsoudas 1970, and
Ross 1967a.

4
See, for instance, Bach 1970, Bresnan 1970, Dougherty 1969, Grinder and
Postal 1971, Jackendoff 1972, Kayne 1971, G. Lakoff 1968, Langacker 1969,
Lees and Klima 1963, and Ross 1967b.

5
See, for instance, with reference to Spanish, Rivero 1971, and Hooper
and Terrell 1974.

6
See, for instance, Mathesius 1928, Firbas 1964, 1966, and Daneš 1967.
Prague school ideas are examined in more detail on the next chapter.

7
Gili y Gaya (1961:86) goes even further, and states that intonation is
part of the 'arte de la declamación', therefore not a grammatical phenomenon at all.

8
Jackendoff (1972:56) draws a distinction between 'subject-oriented' adverbs like cleverly and 'sentence-oriented' adverbs like of course. Our
examples show, however, that the relevant difference must be established
in rhematic terms: adverbs like cleverly combine only with agents which
do not constitute the highest ranking rheme. Reference to the subject
is not particularly useful in this case, since, even though both (1.24)
and (1.25) have a subject, the latter sentence in ungrammatical.

9
We are using the terms subject and direct object in their traditional
meaning. In chapter thirteen, we will make some proposals to reconsider
the traditional definition of these terms.

10
For a similar formulation, see Huckin 1973.

11
For a detailed discussion of the rheme selection hierarchy, see chapter
five.

12
For a detailed discussion of the notion of assertion, see Hooper 1973.

Chapter Two

LINGUISTIC THEORY AND THE STUDY OF WORD ORDER

2.0 Introduction

It would be an understatement to say that word order has not figured prominently among the concerns of grammarians and linguistic theoreticians. No attention was paid to it by Indian, Greek or Roman grammarians, and the situation did not change substantially through the Middle Ages and the Renaissance. Even the seventeenth century grammarians of Port Royal, whose insights in other areas of linguistic theory have been so justly praised by modern transformationalists, have nothing to say about word order, due to their belief that word order simply reflects the natural order of thought processes and, consequently, its study is not part of grammar.[1]

Nor does the study of word order fare any better with modern structuralism. Saussure's conception of langue as an inventory of units and relationships in fact relegates most of syntax to the area of individual variation, parole; and it is a well known fact that American structuralism never developed the theoretical apparatus to deal but with the most superficial aspects of syntax. It is true that interesting typological statements relating to word order have been made by Greenberg (1963), a structuralist, but these statements are based on surface structure, and for the most part do not take into account either more abstract levels of representation or the interrelationships between word order and prosodic phenomena.

2.1 Linguistic theory and the theory of word order

2.1.1 Contribution of the Prague school

The only structuralist school that has devoted some attention to word order is the Prague school, particularly Mathesius (1928), and more recently Firbas (1964, 1966) and Daneš (1967), among others.

Mathesius' major contribution to the study of word order is the idea of the functional sentence perspective, according to which the sentence comprises two parts, the theme, which contains old information, and the rheme, which presents new information. These two parts often correspond to subject and predicate, but that is not always the case. Such correspondence holds, for instance, in a sentence like (2.1),

(2.1) Spring is around the corner.

provided the intonation is normal, that is, with the peak on corner, but it does not hold for a sentence like (2.2) with normal intonation,

(2.2) This argument I can't follow.

where the direct object this argument is the theme and the rest of the sentence the rheme.

According to Mathesius (1928:66), if the theme precedes the rheme, the sentence is said to have an objective order; otherwise, the order is subjective. Thus, both sentences, (2.1) and (2.2), have an objective order if the intonational peak falls on corner and follow respectively. If, on the other hand, the intonational peak falls on spring and argument respectively, the noun phrases spring and this argument become the rheme, and

the rest of the sentence the theme; the order in this case is, of course,
subjective.

Mathesius' ideas have been elaborated on by contemporary linguists
like F. Daneš, J. Dubský (1960), and particularly J. Firbas. These linguists have failed, however, to formulate an explicit theory of word order, valuable though their observations may be, and in some respects
their elaboration of Mathesius' ideas is a step backward. Thus, instead
of Mathesius' dichotomy between theme and rheme, Firbas analyzes the functional perspective of the sentence in terms of degrees of communicative
dynamism, defined as 'the extent to which the sentence element contributes
to the development of the communication, the extent to which, as it were,
it "pushes" the communication forward (Firbas 1966:240).' The scale of
communicative dynamism allows Firbas to distinguish no less than the following five different kinds of elements: rheme proper, rheme, transition,
theme, theme proper.

Firbas' modification of Mathesius' framework stems from the fact
that the theme does not always contain old information. Thus, the following sentence,

(2.3) Mr. Brown has turned out an excellent teacher.

which Firbas analyzes as consisting of theme (Mr. Brown), transition (has
turned out) and rheme (an excellent teacher), may occur either in a context where Mr. Brown is 'old information' or in a context where it is not;
in other words, this sentence may answer either one of the following
questions:

(2.4) What about Mr. Brown?

(2.5) What is it you want to tell me?

Firbas' way out of this dilemma is to say that even though Mr. Brown
is not necessarily old information, it contributes the least to the communication. But it is hard to see what substance this notion of relative
degrees of communicative dynamism might have. One cannot but agree with
Nelson Francis (1966:149) that this kind of analysis is 'marked by a good
deal of arbitrary statement.'

What needs to be done in order to rescue Mathesius' original theme/
rheme dichotomy, while avoiding Firbas' arbitrary concept of communicative
dynamism, is the following:

a) to distinguish between deep and surface structure, and to assume
that the former characterizes elements as either thematic or rhematic.
This means that sentence (2.3) is, in fact, ambiguous: it either derives
from a deep structure where both the subject and the predicate are rhematic, or from one in which only the latter is;

b) to redefine theme and rheme along the following lines (suggested
by Chafe 1974): the theme contains those elements which are assumed by
the speaker to be in the addressee's consciousness; the rheme, those elements which the speaker tries to bring to the addressee's consciousness.

Given this redefinition of the concepts of theme and rheme, it is
hard to imagine how there can be more than two terms: it makes no sense
to assume that a given element is 'more' present in the addressee's consciousness than another.

2.1.2 Bolinger's theory of linear modification

Similar to the Prague school notions on word order is Bolinger's
(1952) principle of linear modification, which says that words are ar-

ranged from left to right in an increasing order of specificity. Thus, for instance, the difference between (2.6) and (2.7)

(2.6) Why did you abruptly back away?

(2.7) Why did you back away abruptly?

is explained in terms of a broad versus a narrow meaning of abruptly in the former and the latter sentence respectively, and the reverse for the meaning of back away. In Bolinger's words, 'the first [sentence] asks essentially "Why did you back away at all?", while the second asks "Why, having decided to back away, did you do it abruptly?" (op. cit. 1120).'

He notices, furthermore, the following asymmetry between these two sentences: 'the first can be contrastive, but only as a whole; we might say Why did you abruptly back away? Why didn't you courteously accept as I wanted you to? The second is contrastive in either part, depending on the stress: Why did you back away abruptly when I told you to dart forward abruptly? and Why did you back away abruptly when I said to do it gradually? When abruptly precedes the verb, it is difficult for contrastive stress to set it off against back away. We should seldom if ever say Why did you abruptly back away when I told you to slowly back away? (op. cit. 1120).'

These are certainly interesting observations, but what Bolinger fails to point out is that his principle of linear modification does not explain the asymmetry just referred to. There is no reason within his theory for back away abruptly and abruptly back away to behave differently except in terms of broad versus narrow meaning. What is needed is a theory that will assign to these sequences a different status independent of linear order. Specifically, the theory must explain why in the phrase back away abruptly it is possible for the speaker to treat either abruptly alone or the whole phrase as 'new' information (i.e. as absent from the addressee's consciousness), whereas in abruptly back away only the verb may be treated as such. The rheme selection hierarchy which will be proposed in this study, together with the linear order rules, constitute an attempt to provide an explanation for these and similar facts.

2.1.3 Contribution of the transformational school

As for the transformational school, its concern with word order falls into two distinct areas. The first one is the question of order in base structures; the second, the problem of 'stylistic reordering.'

Concerning order in base structures, Chomsky (1965:124) has defended the position that base structures are linearly ordered, against proposals by Curry (1961) and Shaumjan and Soboleva (1963) (also later by Staal (1967) and Sanders (1969)) to the effect that they should be considered as unordered set-systems.

The most recent treatment of this question is in Bach (1975), who while concluding that 'the evidence so far supports the idea that underlying structures are ordered' concedes that 'the question must remain open until a whole lot more work has been done (p. 338).'

As for the rules of 'stylistic reordering' Chomsky (1965:126-7) suggests that they 'are not so much rules of grammar as rules of performance.' This position, adopted uncritically by Kiefer (1967:216) in his study on Hungarian word order, among others, is clearly wrong for most cases of so-called stylistic reordering. As this study will make unmistakably clear, a large number of instances involving what has been mistakenly called stylistic reordering follow well defined rules and are by no means subject to the free choice of the speaker.

To give just one example, it would certainly be inadequate to say that the Spanish sentences (2.8) and (2.9) are stylistic variants of each other,

(2.8) Ayer llegó PEDRO.
      'PETER arrived yesterday.'

(2.9) Pedro llegó AYER.
      'Peter arrived YESTERDAY.'

in view of the fact that when they are constituents of larger sentences, the grammar must somehow condition their occurrence to other factors in the larger grammatical context. Thus, the grammar must mark (2.10) as anomalous,

(2.10) *Ayer llegó PEDRO, no ANTEAYER.'
       'PETER arrived yesterday, not the day before YESTERDAY.'

while generating (2.11) and (2.12) as normal sentences.

(2.11) Ayer llegó PEDRO, no MANUEL.
       'PETER arrived yesterday, not MANUEL.'

(2.12) Pedro llegó AYER, no ANTEAYER.
       'Peter arrived YESTERDAY, not the day before YESTERDAY.'

If the difference between (2.10) on the one hand and (2.11) and (2.12) on the other is a matter of grammar, so must be the difference between (2.8) and (2.9).

Both generative semantics (see Lakoff 1969) and Chomsky's (1969, 1970) extended standard theory have recognized the importance of 'old' or 'given' versus 'new' information (using the terms presupposition and focus) in the interpretation of sentences. For Chomsky, this is presumably a modification of his 1965 view just referred to.

In the preceding chapter, we have commented on the inadequacy of the terms focus and presupposition to designate 'new' and 'old' information. Independently of this terminological question, we must examine now the contribution of these two theories to the explanation of word order and sentence stress phenomena.

Lakoff (1969) is not centrally concerned with the problem, and his contribution is limited to the suggestion that the notions of focus and presupposition are part of semantic structure.

Chomsky (1969), on the other hand, argues for a theory where the sentence is divided into focus and presupposition on the basis of information present in the surface structure. His principle for the identification of the focus is as follows:

'The focus is a phrase containing the intonation center;
the presupposition, an expression derived by replacing the
focus by a variable (op. cit. 26).'

Thus, given a sentence like (2.13),

(2.13) Was it an ex-convict with a red SHIRT that he was warned
       to look out for?

any one of the following elements may function as the focus:

(2.14) a. shirt
       b. a red shirt
       c. with a red shirt
       d. an ex-convict with a red shirt

that is, the question may be answered by any of these sentences:

(2.15) a. No, he was warned to look out for an ex-convict with a
          red TIE.
       b. No, he was warned to look out for an ex-convict with a
          CARNATION.
       c. No, he was warned to look out for an ex-convict wearing
          DUNGAREES.
       d. No, he was warned to look out for an AUTOMOBILE salesman.

Although Chomsky's principle will produce the right results in cases
like this, there are other cases where it fails. Hope (1973), for instance, has pointed out that in questions like the following,

(2.16) a. How many people DIED?
       b. Who CAME?
       c. What HAPPENED?
       d. Where is he LIVING?

Chomsky's principle will mistakenly assign the focus to the verb. Thus,
for instance, the presupposition of (2.16a) will be 'how many people X'ed'
instead of the correct 'X people died.'
    This suggests that the assignment of focus is more complicated than
Chomsky's rule would lead us to believe, and it weakens his claim that
focus and presupposition may be determined in surface structure.
    Let us consider a similar example. The question (2.17)

(2.17) Where do your sisters live?

may be answered as follows:

(2.18) MARY lives in CHICAGO; JANE (lives) in New YORK.

where each conjunct has two main stresses, the first one followed by mid-
level pitch and a pause. Chomsky's principle predicts that the possible
focuses for the first conjunct in (2.18) are in Chicago, lives in Chicago,
Mary lives in Chicago, and Mary, but actually the only possible interpretation of this sentence is with focuses on Mary and in Chicago; in
other words, the presupposition is 'X lives in Y.'
    Let us look at the arguments presented by Chomsky in support of
the rule that determines the focus and presupposition from surface
structure information. They basically reduce to the following two:

    a) sentences with the same deep structure may have different focuses;
    b) the focus may be a surface structure constituent which is not a
deep structure constituent.

    I will illustrate the first argument with the following example:
given the questions (2.19),

(2.19) a. Did John give the book to BILL?
       b. Did John give Bill the BOOK?

the answer (2.20) is appropriate only for the former,

(2.20) No, to somebody ELSE.

and the answer (2.21) only for the latter.

(2.21) No, something ELSE.

    Since the sentences in (2.19), Chomsky argues, have the same deep
structure, it follows that focus and presupposition are surface structure

categories. He admits that alternatively these facts could be accounted
for by a theory that assigned focus and presupposition in deep structure,
in which case the deep structures of the sentences in (2.19) would differ. This analysis, however, in Chomsky's opinion is just a notational
variant of the one he proposes.

The crux of the matter is clearly the notion of deep structure. If
it can be shown that that level is defined, independently of focus and
presupposition, as a level that excludes these notions, Chomsky has an
argument. Otherwise, his claim that deep structure excludes focus and
presupposition is vacuous, since deep structure has been defined to begin
with as a level that excludes these notions.

Chomsky's theory would be strengthened by identifying some general
principle from which it follows that the ungrammaticality of strings like
the following

(2.22) a. *John didn't give the book to BILL, but something ELSE.
       b. * John hates it$_i$, and Bill plays the FLUTE$_i$.

is essentially different from other cases. This, I believe, Chomsky has
yet to demonstrate.

Let us now turn to the argument which says that certain elements
which are not deep structure constituents may be surface structure focuses. Chomsky's example is the following,

(2.23) Is John certain to WIN?

which can have any of the following focuses:

(2.24) a. to win
       b. certain to win
       c. is John certain to win

that is, it may be answered by any of the following statements:

(2.25) a. No, John is certain to LOSE.
       b. No, John is likely not even to be NOMINATED.
       c. No, the election will never take PLACE.

Since certain to win is not a deep structure constituent, the argument goes, it must be the case that focus is assigned in surface structure. However, a theory that assigns the focus in deep structure can account for this example simply by allowing each clause to have its own
focus or focuses. Thus, given a tructure like (2.26),

(2.26) [$_S$John win]$_S$ is certain.

the constituents win and certain may be assigned focus status in deep
structure, which is compatible with the fact that question (2.23) may be
answered by (2.25b).

Summing up, it seems that Chomsky's case for determining focus and
presupposition in surface structure is not particularly strong. The alternative analysis of assigning focus and presupposition in deep structure seems just as plausible. This is the course I have followed in this
study. Whether or not it is a notational variant of Chomsky's theory is
still an open question.

2.2 The study of Spanish word order

2.2.1 Traditional grammarians

Among traditional Spanish grammarians, Gili y Gaya (1961) is the one

who has dealt most extensively with word order. His approach, however, is
quite limited due to his disregard of prosodic factors. He states, for
instance, that in a sentence like (2.27),

(2.27) A las siete vendrá Juan.
'At seven John will come.'

the time of John's coming is emphasized, whereas in a sentence like
(2.28),

(2.28) Vendrá Juan a las siete.
'John will come at seven.'

the affirmation of John's coming is emphasized.

If stress and intonation are taken into accout, it is clear that
(2.27) does not necessarily emphasize the time of John's coming. In fact,
if that sentence is pronounced with normal intonation, that is, with the
main stress on Juan, the time of John's coming is certainly not emphasized. Gili y Gaya's statement with respect to sentence (2.27) is adequate only for the version where the main stress goes on the adverbial
expression a las siete. But it is stress, and not word order, which is
responsible for the prominence of this phrase, since it would be just as
prominent if it occurred in final position, provided it carried the main
stress.

Gili y Gaya admits that order is not the only factor which contributes to emphasis, but states that 'acento de intensidad, entonación y
tempo...pertenecen al arte de la Declamación, y caen ya fuera de la Sin-
taxis (op. cit. #70).' Such a narrow view of syntax, which, in fact,
limits itself to the written language, cannot provide the foundation for
an adequate theory of word order. This is made quite clear, for instance,
in the following 'law' suggested by Gili y Gaya (#73): '...the verb cannot
occur without affectation beyond [i.e. to the right of] the second place
[in the sentence].' This principle is offered as an explanation of the
ungrammaticality of sentences like the following:

(2.29) *La mañana hermosa era.
(Cf. La mañana era hermosa.)
'The morning was beautiful.'

(2.30) *El criado una carta trajo para mí.
(El criado trajo una carta para mí.)
'The servant brought a letter for me.'

It is not hard, however, to find sentences which violate Gili y Gaya's principle:

(2.31) Esta carta el criado la trajo para mí.
'This letter the servant brought for me.'

(2.32) Si no haces la tarea, el profesor te mata.
'If you don't do your homework, the teacher will kill you.'

The facts related to word order are too complex to be reduced to such
simple principles. Besides, any attempt at an explanation which ignores
the relationship between order and prosodic factors is bound to be ina-
quate.

In all fairness to Gili y Gaya, however, his concern with word order
must be applauded. He is in fact one of the few Spanish traditional grammarians to devote any attention to this problem. Neither Bello (1847) nor
Lenz (1944) deal with the problem extensively, and as for the Real Acade-

mia Española, only its new Esbozo (1973) devotes a chapter to word order, taken almost literally from Gili y Gaya.

2.2.2 American structuralists

Among the linguists working within the American structuralist tradition, Henry Kahane is the one who has contributed the most to the study of Spanish word order, both through his own work (Kahane and Kahane 1950) and through the work of his students (for instance, Ringo 1954, and Mc-Williams 1954).

Just like Gili y Gaya, these linguists approach the description of word order independently of prosodic factors, which renders their analysis just as limited. This limitation is shown, for instance, in the fact that in Kahane and Kahane (1950), the following two sentences are considered as free variants:

(2.33) a. Se enojó Ramón.
       b. Ramón se enojó.
          'Ramón got angry.'

In view of the discussion presented in chapter one of this study, it should be clear that this is an inadequate analysis. Limiting ourselves to normal intonation, with the main stress on Ramón and enojó respectively sentence (2.33a) may answer a question like (2.34),

(2.34) ¿Quién se enojó?
       'Who got angry?'

whereas sentence (2.33b) answers questions (2.35) and (2.36), but not (2.34).

(2.35) ¿Qué pasó con Ramón?
       'What about Ramón?'

(2.36) ¿Qué pasó?
       'What happened?'

Quite clearly, sentences (2.33a) and (2.33b) are not equivalent.

Let us see another example. In the analysis of sentences like (2.37) and (2.38),

(2.37) Si Alberto no va, irá Luis.
       'If Alberto doesn't go, Luis will.'

(2.38) A pesar de que tenía luto, bailó María.
       'In spite of her being in mourning, Mary danced.'

it is suggested that the final position of the subject in the second clause is related to the fact that there is an adverbial expression in initial position, but no mention is made of the fact that the normal intonation of these sentences is different: while (2.37) requires the main stress to go on Luis, in (2.38) it must fall on bailó, or of the fact that the unmarked order for (2.38), despite the presence of the adverbial in initial position, is as follows:

(2.39) A pesar de que tenía luto, María BAILÓ.
       'In spite of her being in mourning, Mary DANCED.'

These facts indicate that the final position of the subject cannot be explained in terms of an initial adverbial expression, but that the position of all elements depends on the rhematic structure of the sentence.

2.2.3 Studies related to Prague-school ideas

The most insightful studies of Spanish word order are those directly or indirectly related to the Prague school notions of old and new information, for instance, Bolinger (1954, 1954-5), Dubský (1960), and Hatcher (1956). Stiehm has also recently dealt with the problem from this point of view.

In these studies, order is approached in relation to prosodic factors and context, which leads to an analysis far more satisfactory than other approaches. What limits the validity of these studies, however, is their lack of explicitness.

Since the present study is an attempt to convert Prague-school ideas into explicit rules of word order, no further discussion of these ideas is necessary at this point.

2.2.4 The transformational approach

We are not aware of any transformationally oriented study of Spanish word order. The analysis suggested by Hadlich (1971:108), which, on the basis of an underlying order, allows the free reordering of any element by means of a rule curiously labelled TOPICALIZATION, is clearly inadequate. On the one hand, this rule generates ungrammatical sentences like (2.40),

(2.40) *La carta Juan leyó.
'The letter John read.'

and on the other it assigns the same underlying structure to sentences like (2.41) and (2.42),

(2.41) Empezó la RESISTENCIA.
'The RESISTANCE started.'

(2.42) La resistencia EMPEZÓ.
'The resistance STARTED.'

which, in view of the facts presented in chapter one, is inadequate.

Although an introductory work like Hadlich 1971 cannot be expected to deal with any one aspect of Spanish grammar in depth, it should be pointed out that with respect to word order its inadequacy is fundamental, not a matter of detail.

FOOTNOTES TO CHAPTER TWO

[1]See Lancelot et al. (1660). See also Chomsky (1965:8ff) for further discussion of the views of Port Royal grammarians.

Chapter Three

TOWARDS A NEW THEORY

In chapter one, we demonstrated the semantic and syntactic relevance of the concepts theme and rheme, defined respectively as information which the speaker assumes to be present in the addressee's consciousness and as information assumed by the speaker to be absent from the addressee's consciousness.

We must now begin to identify the factors necessary for an explicit
theory of word order and sentential stress. In view of the preliminary
discussion presented in chapter one, it would seem that the following
factors must be reckoned with: a) rheme selection; b) linear order of
theme and rheme.

3.1 Rheme selection

Any element of semantic structure may function as a rheme,[1] but the
selection of one or another element is not indifferent. Thus, for instance,
with a verb denoting 'beginning', as Hatcher (1956) has noted, the subject takes priority over the verb as a possible rheme. Thus, a sentence
like (3.1) may be said to be normal with respect to rheme selection,

(3.1) Empezó la RESISTENCIA.
      'The RESISTANCE started.'

in contrast with a sentence like (3.2).

(3.2) La resistencia EMPEZÓ.
      'The resistance STARTED.'

A sentence with normal rheme selection has greater contextual freedom than one with abnormal rheme selection. It is clear, for instance,
that (3.1) has more contextual freedom than (3.2), since it can answer
both (3.3) and (3.4),

(3.3) ¿Qué empezó?
      'What started?'

(3.4) ¿Qué pasó?
      'What happened?'

whereas (3.2) answers only (3.5).

(3.5) ¿Qué pasó con la resistencia?
      'What about the resistance?'

Putting it differently, sentence (3.1), where the highest ranking
element is in final position and carries the main stress, allows two different interpretations: one in which only the highest ranking element is
the rheme, and one in which the whole sentence is rhematic; sentence (3.2),
on the other hand, where the highest ranking element is neither in final
position nor does it carry the main stress, allows only the interpretation
where the final element, and nothing else, is rhematic.

Informally, we will say that sentences like (3.1) show typical rheme
selection, and that sentences like (3.2), where the rheme selection hierarchy is violated, show atypical rheme selection.

A theory of word order and main stress placement must include a rheme
selection hierarchy sufficiently rich to distinguish typical from atypic-

al rheme selections for any type of sentence. We will propose such a
hierarchy further on.

3.2 Rheme ordering

The second factor that a theory of word order and sentential stress
must take into account if the linear distribution of theme and rheme.
Both in (3.1) and in (3.2), the theme (or the highest ranking rheme
if there is more than one) occurs in final position. We will say that
this is the normal linear arrangement. In addition, however, there is an
emphatic order, which is the reverse of normal order,[2] shown, for instance, in sentences like the following:

(3.6) La RESISTENCIA empezó.
      'The RESISTANCE started.'

(3.7) EMPEZÓ la resistencia.
      'The resistance STARTED.'

Just as sentences with typical rheme selection have more contextual
freedom than sentences with atypical rheme selection, sentences with
normal linear order have greater contextual freedom than sentences with
emphatic word order. Specifically, emphatic sentences are restricted to
assertive contexts, that is, they occur either as independent sentences
or embedded under assertive verbs like decir 'to say', but not embedded
under non-assertive verbs like lamentar 'to regret'. Sentences with normal word order, on the other hand, are not subject to this limitation.
Thus, for instance, sentence (3.1) may occur in all of the following contexts,

(3.8) Empezó la RESISTENCIA.
      'The RESISTANCE started.'

(3.9) Dicen que empezó la RESISTENCIA.
      'They say the RESISTANCE started.'

(3.10) Lamento que empezara la RESISTENCIA.
       'I regret the RESISTANCE started.'

while sentences like (3.6) occur in only two of these contexts, namely
those that are 'assertive':

(3.11) La RESISTENCIA empezó.
       'The RESISTANCE started.'

(3.12) Dicen que la RESISTENCIA empezó.
       'They say the RESISTANCE started.'

(3.13) *Lamento que la RESISTENCIA empezara.
       'I regret the RESISTANCE started.'

Summing up, a theory of word order and sentential stress must account
for the differences between the following types of sentences:

	Rheme selection	Linear order
(3.1) Empezó la RESISTENCIA.	Typical	Normal
(3.2) La resistencia EMPEZÓ.	Atypical	Normal
(3.6) La RESISTENCIA empezó.	Typical	Emphatic
(3.7) EMPEZÓ la resistencia.	Atypical	Emphatic

3.3 Rheme selection and syntactic structure

It may be useful to point out that what determines whether the rheme selection of a sentence is typical or atypical is not its syntactic but its semantic structure. I will support this statement with a couple of examples, the first one showing two sentences with the same syntactic structure and different rhematic hierachy, the second one showing the opposite case.
Sentence (3.14)

(3.14) La resistencia fracasó.
       'The resistance failed.'

shows the same syntactic structure as that of the sentences discussed above with the verb _empezar_ 'to begin', yet its rhematic hierarchy is different. Thus, in contrast with the sentences with _empezar_, the typical rheme selection for this sentence is that of (3.15), not that of (3.16),

(3.15) La resistencia FRACASÓ.
       'The resistance FAILED.'

(3.16) Fracasó la RESISTENCIA.
       'The RESISTANCE failed.'

since sentence (3.15) may answer either (3.17) or (3.18),

(3.17) ¿Qué pasó con la resistencia?
       'What about the resistance?'

(3.18) ¿Qué pasó?
       'What happened?'

whereas sentence (3.16) may answer only (3.19).

(3.19) ¿Qué fracasó?
       'What failed?'

This different behavior is no doubt due to the different semantic features of the verbs in question. Anticipating somewhat the results of this study, we will say that there are some verbs, denoting beginning, appearance, existence, etc. (see Hatcher 1956) which seem to have a 'presentational' function and which give rhematic priority to their subjects. Other verbs, like _fracasar_ 'to fail', tend to treat their subjects as themes.
Before presenting our second example, it should be pointed out that there is a difference between what we are calling typical rheme selection and what would constitute the most appropriate rheme selection in a given context. Thus, for instance, in the middle of a conversation about the resistance, (3.2) would be a more appropriate sentence than (3.1).

(3.2) La resistencia EMPEZÓ.
      'The resistance STARTED.'

(3.1) Empezó la RESISTENCIA.
      'The RESISTANCE started.'

By the same token, in the middle of a conversation about failure, (3.16) would be a more appropriate sentence than (3.15).

(3.16) Fracasó la RESISTENCIA.
       'The RESISTANCE failed.'

(3.15) La resistencia FRACASÓ.
'The resistance FAILED.'

However, in the absence of a relevant context, for instance, at the beginning of a conversation, (3.1) and (3.15) are appropriate, and (3.2) and (3.16) are not. Consequently, we consider the former as sentences with typical rheme selection.

Let us consider now the following two sentences with a different syntactic structure but identical rhematic hierarchy:

(3.20) María cree que va a llover.
'Mary thinks it's going to rain.'

(3.21) A María le parece que va a llover.
'It seems to Mary that it's going to rain.'

Starting with sentence (3.20), we notice that the highest ranking element for the purpose of rheme selection is the clause que va a llover 'it's going to rain', since the following version

(3.22) María cree que va a LLOVER.
'Mary thinks it's going to RAIN.'

shows more contextual freedom than either (3.23) or (3.24).

(3.23) Que va a llover cree MARÍA.
'MARY thinks it's going to rain.'

(3.24) Que va a llover María lo CREE.
'Mary THINKS it's going to rain.'

In other words, sentence (3.22) answers all of these questions:

(3.25) ¿Qué cree María?
'What does Mary think?'

(3.26) ¿Qué hay con María?
'What about Mary?'

(3.27) ¿Qué hay?
'What's up?'

whereas sentences (3.23) and (3.24) answer a more restricted range of questions.

Now, since the syntactic function of the clause que va a llover is different in sentences (3.20) and (3.21), we would expect its behavior with respect to rheme selection to be also different. But it is not. Just as with (3.20), the typical rheme selection for (3.21) is represented by a version where the clause que va a llover takes priority over the other elements: (3.28) has greater contextual freedom than either (3.29) or (3.30).

(3.28) A María le parece que va a LLOVER.
'It seems to Mary it's going to RAIN.'

(3.29) Que va a llover le parece a MARÍA.
'It seems to MARY it's going to rain.'

(3.30) Que va a llover a María le PARECE.
'It SEEMS to Mary it's going to rain.'

In order to explain this fact, one must go beyond the syntactic structure of the sentences involved. It is at the semantic level that the similarity between these two sentences is revealed. Thus, in both of

them there is an experiencer (María) and a patient (que va a llover)[3] and
in both of them the patient has priority for the purposes of rheme selection, regardless of the fact that syntactically the patient is subject in
one case and direct object in the other.

Summing up, the rheme selection hierarchy is determined by the semantic structure of the sentence. This explains the fact that two intran-
sitive verbs like empezar 'to begin' and fracasar 'to fail' impose a different rheme selection to the sentences where they occur, as well as the
fact that the verbs creer 'to think' and parecer 'to seem', which have
different syntactic properties but similar semantic properties, assign
rhematic priority to the same element, namely the patient clause.

3.4 Order and sentence stress

Looking now in more detail at the problem of linear order, there are
two facts which any theory must account for: first, the elements appearing to the right of the main sentential stress are always interpreted as
thematic; second, the elements preceding the main sentential stress may
be interpreted as theme or rheme according to their place in the rheme
selection hierarchy.

The first fact is clearly shown by sentences like the following,

(3.6) La RESISTENCIA empezó.
      'The RESISTANCE started.'

(3.7) EMPEZÓ la resistencia.
      'The resistance STARTED.'

(3.31) La RESISTENCIA fracasó.
       'The RESISTANCE failed.'

(3.32) FRACASÓ la resistencia.
       'The resistance FAILED.'

(3.33) Que va a LLOVER cree María.
       'Mary thinks it's going to RAIN.'

(3.34) Que va a LLOVER le parece a María.
       'It seems to Mary that it's going to RAIN.'

where the elements to the right of the main sentential stress cannot be
interpreted but as 'given' information, that is, theme.

As for the elements which precede the main stress, notice that whereas in (3.1) and (3.15) they may be interpreted either as theme or as
rheme,

(3.1) Empezó la RESISTENCIA.
      'The RESISTANCE started.'

(3.15) La resistencia FRACASÓ.
       'The resistance FAILED.'

in (3.2) and (3.16) they may only be interpreted as theme.

(3.2) La resistencia EMPEZÓ.
      'The resistance STARTED.'

(3.16) Fracasó la RESISTENCIA.
       'The RESISTANCE failed.'

What distinguishes the first from the second pair of sentences is
that in the former the element which precedes the sentential stress ranks

lower in the rhematic hierarchy than the one on which the stress falls.
From this observation we deduce the following principle:

(3.35) The elements which precede the main sentential stress may
be interpreted as theme or rheme if they rank lower than
the element on which the stress falls; otherwise, they are
interpreted as theme.

This principle is corroborated by sentences like the following:

(3.22) María cree que va a LLOVER.
'Mary thinks it's going to RAIN.'

(3.28) A María le parece que va a LLOVER.
'It seems to Mary that it's going to RAIN.'

where the material preceding the main stress may be interpreted as theme
or rheme, in contrast with sentences like (3.23) and (3.29),

(3.23) Que va a llover cree MARÍA.
'MARY thinks it's going to rain.'

(3.29) Que va a llover le parece a MARÍA.
'It seems to MARY that it's going to rain.'

where the elements preceding the main stress can only be interpreted as
theme.

3.5 Conclusions

Summing up the discussion of this chapter, a theory of word order
and sentential stress must distinguish on the one hand between typical
and atypical rheme selection, and on the other between normal and emphatic linear order.

The difference between typical and atypical rheme selection depends
on a rhematic hierarchy based on the semantic structure of the sentence.

Finally, our theory must assign the main sentential stress to an
element determined by the rhematic hierarchy, and must predict the thematic or rhematic interpretation of the remaining elements.

FOOTNOTES TO CHAPTER THREE

[1]This element need not be a major constituent of the sentence. Thus, one of the possible underlying structures of (i)

> (i) María dice que está escribiendo una novela.
> 'Mary says she is writing a novel.'

has una novela 'a novel' as the only rheme.

I will not attempt a more precise statement as to which elements are eligible for rhematic status. Unmodified noun phrases such as the ones underlined in (ii) and (iii) seem to function only as rhemes.

> (ii) Hombres y mujeres unieron sus voces en protesta por la discriminación contra la mujer.
> 'Men and women joined their voices in protest of the discrimination against women.'

> (iii) Al amanecer gruesas gotas de lluvia cayeron sobre la tierra (Rulfo 76).
> 'At dawn thick drops of rain fell on the ground.'

It is not clear just how this fact is to be incorporated formally into the grammar.

[2]Besides this general rule, there are special rules which take into account other factors, for instance, the internal complexity of the sentence constituents. We will deal with these cases later.

[3]We discuss these concepts in the next chapter.

Chapter Four

SEMANTIC STRUCTURE

We have established that the rhematic hierarchy depends on the semantic structure of the sentence. In order to give substance to this claim, we must make explicit what we understand by semantic structure.[1]

We assume that a sentence consists of a <u>nucleus</u> or <u>core</u> plus optional <u>adjuncts</u>. The core includes a <u>predicate</u>, which is normally a surface structure verb, but which may also be represented by other parts of speech, mainly nouns and adjectives, and one or more <u>arguments</u>.

In the following sentences, for instance,

(4.1) Morirá el dictador.
      'The dictator will die.'

(4.2) El dictador es cruel.
      'The dictator is cruel.'

(4.3) El dictador es general.
      'The dictator is a general.'

the predicate is, respectively, the verb <u>morirá</u>, the adjective <u>cruel</u>, and the noun <u>general</u>. The verb <u>ser</u> 'to be' is not part of semantic structure, but is inserted transformationally as a tense and person morpheme carrier. All these sentences include in addition an argument, <u>el dictador</u>.

With other predicates, as in the following examples, two, three, four, and even five arguments may occur:

(4.4) <u>El dictador</u> - sofocó - <u>la rebelión</u>.
      'The dictator - crushed - the rebellion.'

(4.5) <u>El pueblo</u> - odia - <u>al dictador</u>.
      'The people - hate - the dictator.'

(4.6) <u>El dictador</u> - le quitó - <u>la libertad</u> - <u>al pueblo</u>.
      'The dictator - took away - freedom - from the people.'

(4.7) <u>El pueblo</u> - le dio - <u>un gran triunfo</u> - <u>a Allende</u>.
      'The people - gave - Allende - a great victory.'

(4.8) <u>Juan</u> - le cambió - <u>un fusil</u> - <u>a Pedro</u> - <u>por unos libros</u>.
      'John - gave - Peter - a gun - for some books.'

(4.9) <u>Pedro</u> - le vendió - <u>los libros</u> - <u>a María</u> - <u>por poco dinero</u>.
      'Peter - sold - the books - to Mary - for little money.'

(4.10) <u>El dictador</u> - le compró - <u>a los Estados Unidos</u> - <u>cinco aviones de guerra</u> - <u>para Chile</u> - <u>en quinientos mil dólares</u>.
       'The dictator - bought - from the United States - five war planes - for Chile - for five hundred thousand dollars.'

Each argument expresses a particualr relation with respect to the predicate. Sentence (4.4) illustrate the two most basic types of arguments: the agent (<u>el dictador</u>) and the patient (la rebelión).

An <u>agent</u> denotes an animate being which performs an action. A <u>patient</u> denotes something which is in a particular state or which is changing its state. In (4.4), the agent corresponds to the surface subject and the patient to the surface object. This correlation, however, does not always hold. Thus, in (4.1),

(4.1) Morirá el dictador.
     'The dictator will die.'

the surface subject is not an agent but a patient.

The occurrence of certain adverbs like deliberadamente 'deliberately' and con ganas 'with enthusiasm' may be used as a diagnostic test for the presence of an agent: they can occur, for instance, with a sentence like (4.4) but not with one like (4.1).

The fact that this type of adverbial cannot be added to the sentences in (4.11) shows that they do not have an agent either.

(4.11) a. El dictador sabe que la oposición es fuerte.
          'The dictator knows that the opposition is strong.'

      b. El dictador no conoce sus limitaciones.
         'The dictator does not know his limitations.'

      c. El pueblo no olvidará los crímenes del dictador.
         'The people will not forget the dictator's crimes.'

In these sentences, the subject noun phrase is an experiencer, that is, someone who is mentally disposed in a certain way. The experiencer may also appear as a surface indirect object, as in (4.12).

(4.12) a. El líder le recordó al pueblo los crímenes del dictador.
          'The leader reminded the people of the dictator's crimes.'

      b. El periodista mostró al público las pruebas de la intervención de la CIA.
         'The newspaperman showed the public the proofs of the CIA's intervention.'

The surface indirect object is not to be identified with the experiencer in all cases, however. Thus, in (4.13) it is a beneficiary, that is, someone who 'benefits' (in a broad sense) from what the sentence predicates.

(4.13) a. Allende le dio esperanza al pueblo.
          'Allende gave the people hope.'

      b. A un guardia le rompieron una pierna.
         'They broke a guard's leg.'

With verbs related to possession or lack thereof, the surface subject is normally a possessor, as in (4.14).

(4.14) a. El general tiene muchos esbirros.
          'The general has many lackeys.'

      b. El agente perdió unos documentos compremetedores.
         'The agent lost some compromising documents.'

With verbs like perder 'to lose', the possessor may also appear as a surface indirect object, as in (4.15).

(4.15) Al agente se le perdieron unos documentos comprometedores.
       'The agent lost some compromising documents.'

Notice that when the 'object' of perder is not a concrete object, the construction can only be parallel to (4.14b), not to (4.15):

(4.16) a. El pueblo perdió la libertad.
      b. *Al pueblo se le perdió la libertad.
        'The people lost their freedom.'

This surface phenomenon seems to correlate with the fact that in (4.16a), the subject is better interpreted as an experiencer than as a possessor. [2]
The sentences in (4.17) illustrate <u>instruments</u>, that is, objects which play a role in bringing about a process but which are not its main instigator.

(4.17) a. El dictador sofocó la rebelión <u>con tanques</u>.
        'The dictator crushed the rebellion with tanks.'

      b. El pueblo fue amenazado <u>con prisión y tortura</u>.
        'The people were threatened with prison and torture.'

If no agent is present, a <u>cause</u> may appear as a surface subject, as in (4.18).

(4.18) <u>Las balas</u> atemorizaron al pueblo.
      'The bullets frightened the people.'

Natural forces are a common type of cause, as in (4.19).

(4.19) <u>Los truenos</u> atemorizaron a la gente.
      'Thunder frightened the people.'

The sentences in (4.20) illustrate <u>complements</u>.

(4.20) a. Neruda vivió <u>una vida revolucionaria</u>.
        'Neruda lived a revolutionary life.'

      b. La guerra costó <u>muchas vidas</u>.
        'The war cost many lives.'

      c. La libertad vale <u>muchos sacrificios</u>.
        'Freedom is worth many sacrifices.'

      d. La historia, con toda justicia, llamará <u>héroe</u> a Allende.
        'History will justly call Allende a hero.'

The verbs in these sentences describe an action which implies a related nominal concept. Thus, living implies a life, <u>costar</u> and <u>valer</u> imply a nominal element denoting a price, and the verb <u>llamar</u> one denoting a name.
We will now illustrate a pair of correlative arguments: <u>source</u> and <u>target</u>. They denote, respectively, the point in space or time where the action denoted by the verb may be thought to originate, and the point in space or time which the action points to. They both occur in sentences like the following:

(4.21) María viajó <u>de Quito</u> (source) <u>a Lima</u> (target) en autobús.
      'Mary travelled from Quito to Lima by bus.'

(4.22) El doctor atiende <u>de lunes</u> (source) <u>a viernes</u> (target).
      'The doctor is in from Monday to Friday.'

The following sentences contain additional examples of sources:

(4.23) A don Fermín le extrajeron tres balas <u>de las piernas</u> (Arguedas II.271).
      'They extracted three bullets from don Fermín's legs.'

(4.24) El dictador les compró aviones de guerra <u>a los Estados Unidos</u>.
'The dictator bought war planes from the United States.'

Other examples of targets are the following:

(4.25) Los dos jinetes volvieron la cabeza <u>hacia la cárcel</u> (Arguedas
II.46).
'The two riders turned their heads toward the jail.'

(4.26) <u>Para usted</u> ya no tengo ni un centavo (Arguedas II.19).
'For you I don't even have a cent any more.'

(4.27) Al niño lo llevaremos <u>a Lahuaymarca</u> (Arguedas II.262).
'The child we'll take to Lahuaymarca.'

(4.28) El tirano gobernará <u>hasta que el pueblo se rebele</u>.
'The tyrant will rule until the people rebel.'

The distinction between source and beneficiary allows us to account
for the ambiguity of sentences like (4.29).

(4.29) Le compré un libro <u>a mi amigo</u>.

If the underlined phrase indicates a source, the meaning is 'I bought
a book from my friend'; it it is a beneficiary, the meaning is 'I bought a
book for my friend.'

Let us now consider the following copulative sentences:

(4.30) a. El dictador es cruel.
'The dictator is cruel.'

b. El dictador es general.
'The dictator is a general.'

c. El dictador está en su oficina.
'The dictator is in his office.'

d. El golpe fue en el mes de la patria.
'The coup was during the month of the fatherland.'

e. El dictador es un general.
'The dictator is a general.'

f. El dictador es Pinochet.
'The dictator is Pinochet.'

Sentences (4.30a) and (4.30b), as has already been stated, consist
of one argument, <u>el dictador</u>, and a predicate, <u>cruel</u> and <u>general</u> respectively, the verb <u>ser</u> being considered an empty tense and person carrier.
Notice that the noun <u>general</u> in (4.30b) is used non-referentially, that is,
it does not identify a person, but only describes him. This contrasts with
the use of the phrase <u>un general</u> in (4.30e), which does refer to an individual. This latter sentence, consequently, consists of two arguments, <u>el
dictador</u> and <u>un general</u>, and no predicate, the verb <u>ser</u> being just a person
and tense morpheme carrier as in (4.30a) and (4.30b).[3] The same is true of
(4.30c), (4.30d) and (4.30f), in all of which the noun to the right of the
copula is used referentially and constitutes a separate argument.

We must now determine what kinds of arguments occur in copulative
sentences. The arguments to the right of the copula do not seem to fit
the description of any of the types presented so far. The one in (4.30c),
for obvious reasons, will be referred to as <u>location</u>; that in (4.30d) as
<u>time</u>; and those in (4.30e) and (4.30f) as <u>identifiers</u>.[4] The subject of
these sentences is, of course, a patient.

Summing up, we have identified the following kinds of arguments: agent, patient, experiencer, beneficiary, possessor, instrument, cause, complement, source, target, location, time, and identifier. These, together with the predicate, constitute the semantic core of the sentence.

Let us now examine the notion of <u>adjunct</u>. In contrast with arguments, which are severely restricted by the type of predicate, adjuncts occur quite freely with any type of predicate. Thus, for instance, with a predicate like <u>caer</u> 'to fall', a patient is required, and a source and a target may occur optionally, as in the following sentence:

(4.31) El país [patient] cayó (de la democracia [source] a la dictadura [target]).
'The country fell (from democracy to dictatorship).'

but no agent or experiencer is allowed.

On the other hand, a predicate like <u>asesinar</u> 'to murder' requires an agent and a patient, and it may optionally take an instrument, but it does not allow a source or a target.

However, an adjunct like <u>en septiembre</u> 'in September' may occur freely with either one of these two predicates:

(4.32) a. En septiembre, el país cayó de la democracia a la dictadura.
'In September, the country fell from democracy to dictatorship.'

b. En septiembre, el presidente fue asesinado por los traidores.
'In September, the president was murdered by the traitors.'

Since time and location have been identified as arguments, the question arises as to how they differ from adjuncts denoting time and location. In the case of a sentence like (4.33),

(4.33) El caudillo vive en París.
'The caudillo lives in Paris.'

the locative phrase must be considered to be an argument because without it the sentence would be incomplete. On the other hand, the locative phrase in (4.32) is perfectly dispensable, which means it is an adjunct. It is possible, then, for elements of the same type to be either arguments or adjuncts, depending on their relationship to the predicate. It is also possible for a sentence to have two elements of the same type, one as adjunct, the other as argument. An example of this is (4.34),

(4.34) En Chile, hay un dictador en el poder.
'In Chile, there is a dictator in power.'

where the first locative phrase is an adjunct and the second an argument.

This concludes our discussion of semantic structure. It is admittedly very sketchy and tentative, and is offered here only as a necessary point of departure for the operation of the rules of rheme and topic selection and distribution, which constitute the core of this study.

FOOTNOTES TO CHAPTER FOUR

[1] My concept of semantic structure owes a great deal to Chafe (1970), Fillmore (1968, 1971), and Halliday (1967-8).

[2] In other words, _possessor_ seems to be appropriate for cases of literal possession or loss thereof, whereas figurative possession or loss thereof, as in (4.16a), is better analyzed in terms of an experiencer.

[3] The lack of an independent semantic status of _ser_ is shown by the fact that it cannot constitute a rheme by itself, as illustrated by the ungrammaticality of (i),

> (i) *Un general el dictador ES.
>   'A general the dictator IS.'
>   (Cf. La carta Pedro la RECIBIÓ.
>   'The letter, Peter RECEIVED it.')

and by the fact that it cannot be interchanged with the patient, as shown by the ungrammaticality of (ii).

> (ii) *Es el dictador un GENERAL.
>   (Cf. Escribió Pedro una CARTA.)

[4] For an enlightening discussion of the concept _identifier_, see Halliday (1967-8).

Chapter Five

THE RHEME-SELECTION HIERARCHY

5.1 Rheme assignment

In this chapter, we will deal with the problem of rheme selection.

If we analyze the theme/rheme opposition in terms of a binary feature rheme which may be positively ('rheme') or negatively ('theme') specified, and if we assume that such a feature is part of semantic structure, it is possible to formulate the following very general rule of rheme selection:

(5.1) RHEME ASSIGNMENT (OBLIGATORY)

$$\left\{ [\text{+rheme}], \quad X \right\}$$
$$1 \qquad 2 \rightarrow$$
$$\emptyset \qquad \begin{bmatrix} 2 \\ 1 \end{bmatrix}$$

Condition: X is any element in semantic structure.

In addition to this rule, we assume a general convention that assigns the feature [-rheme] to any element which has not been specified [+rheme] by rule (5.1). This rule and this convention generate rhematic structures, that is, structures which specify which elements are considered 'given' ([-rheme]) and which 'new' ([+rheme]). Thus, given semantic structure (5.2),

$$(5.2) \left\{ \begin{array}{lll} [\text{+rheme}], & \text{empezó}, & \text{la resistencia} \\ & \text{Predicate} & \text{Patient} \\ & \text{'started'} & \text{'the resistance'} \end{array} \right\}$$

the following rhematic structures are generated:

$$(5.3) \left\{ \begin{array}{ll} \text{empezó}, & \text{la resistencia} \\ \text{Predicate} & \text{Patient} \\ [\text{-rheme}] & [\text{+rheme}] \end{array} \right\}$$

$$(5.4) \left\{ \begin{array}{ll} \text{empezó}, & \text{la resistencia} \\ \text{Predicate} & \text{Patient} \\ [\text{+rheme}] & [\text{+rheme}] \end{array} \right\}$$

$$(5.5) \left\{ \begin{array}{ll} \text{empezó}, & \text{la resistencia} \\ \text{Predicate} & \text{Patient} \\ [\text{+rheme}] & [\text{-rheme}] \end{array} \right\}$$

Since rule (5.1) is obligatory, the following rhematic structure is not generated:

$$(5.6) \left\{ \begin{array}{ll} \text{empezó}, & \text{la resistencia} \\ \text{Predicate} & \text{Patient} \\ [\text{-rheme}] & [\text{-rheme}] \end{array} \right\}$$

This corresponds to the fact that the addressee always takes some part of the sentence to be intended as new information.

Rhematic structures (5.3) and (5.4) are related to surface structure (5.7).

(5.7) Empezó la RESISTENCIA.
'The RESISTANCE started.'

Rhematic structure (5.3) is also related to surface structure (5.8).

(5.8) La RESISTENCIA empezó.
'The RESISTANCE started.'

This corresponds to the fact, noted in the previous chapter, that elements preceding the main stress may be interpreted as theme or rheme, provided they do not outrank the element carrying the stress, whereas elements following the main stress may only be interpreted as theme.

Rhematic structure (5.5) is related to surface structure (5.9) and (5.10).

(5.9) La resistencia EMPEZÓ.
'The resistance STARTED.'

(5.10) EMPEZÓ la resistencia.
'The resistance STARTED.'

The rules of linear order and assignment of sentential stress which relate rhematic and surface structures will be discussed in later chapters.

Now, since rule (5.1) does not distinguish between typical and atypical rheme selection, it is necessary to establish a separate rheme selection hierarchy which will do so. This hierarchy is formally what Perlmutter (1971) has called a surface structure constraint, but in addition, as we will show, it plays an essential role in the application of some linear order rules.

Tentatively, let us assume the following rheme selection hierarchy:

(5.11) RHEME SELECTION HIERARCHY (TENTATIVE)

1. Patient

2. Predicate denoting 'beginning', 'existence', 'appearance', etc.

Let us also postulate the following definition of <u>violation</u> of the rheme selection hierarchy (henceforth RSH):

(5.12) A structure violates the RSH if X is [-rheme] and Y is [+rheme], and X ranks higher than Y in the RSH.

Given our RSH and the definition of violation, we determine that out of all the rhematic structures generated from semantic structure (5.2), only (5.5) violates the RSH.

Our grammar thus accounts for the difference between typical and atypical rheme selection. Specifically, it distinguishes between the 'marked' structure (5.5) which occurs in restricted contexts, and the rest of the structures which occur in a wider variety of contexts.

5.2 Two-argument sentences

Let us now examine some sentences with two arguments for the purpose of determining their RSH. Eventually, all the different RSH's must be reduced to one, but for expository purposes we will proceed gradually.

Let us examine first some sentences with an agent and a patient, like the following:

(5.13) a. Ella (ag) está procurando enseñarte (pat) (Naranjo 11).
'She is trying to teach you.'

b. Voy a Ø (ag) escribir una novela (pat) (Naranjo 9).
'I'm going to write a novel.'

   c. ...dicen los periódicos (ag) que nuestros servicios no
      sirven para nada (pat) (Naranjo 24).
      '...the newspapers say that our services are good for
      nothing.'

   d. Hace usted (ag) un mal negocio (pat) (Naranjo 95).
      'You're making a bad business transaction.'

When these sentences are pronounced with the main stress on the right-
most constituent, the following rhematic interpretations are possible:
A) rhematic patient;
B) rhematic patient and predicate;
C) the whole sentence is rhematic.
In other words, these sentences may answer questions like (5.14)
(case A),

   (5.14) a. ¿Qué está procurando hacer ella?
        'What is she trying to do?'

       b. ¿Qué vas a escribir?
        'What are you going to write?'

questions like (5.15) (case B),

   (5.15) a. ¿Qué hace ella?
        'What is she doing?'

       b. ¿Qué vas a hacer tú?
        'What are you going to do?'

or questions like (5.16) (case C).

   (5.16) ¿Qué pasa?
       'What's up?'

This suggests the following RSH for these sentences:

(5.17) RHEME SELECTION HIERARCHY (TENTATIVE)

    1. Patient

    2. Predicate

    3. Agent

Besides accounting for the triple interpretation of the sentences in
(5.13), this hierarchy explains that should the patient be predictable,
for instance, if it denoted the addressee, the predicate would have rhematic priority over the agent. Thus, it accounts for the fact that the sentences in (5.18)

   (5.18) a. El director lo LLAMA (Naranjo 88).
        'The director is CALLING you.'

       b. El señor director lo ha estado BUSCANDO (Naranjo 116).
        'The director has been LOOKING for you.'

allow two interpretations, one with the predicate as rheme and one with
the predicate and the agent as rheme; in other words, these sentences
answer questions like (5.19) or questions like (5.20).

   (5.19) ¿Qué hace el director?
       'What is the director doing?'

   (5.20) ¿Qué pasa?
       'What's up?'

On the other hand, if the main stress falls on the agent, for instance, as in (5.21),

> (5.21) Lo llama el DIRECTOR.
> 'The DIRECTOR is calling you.'

the only interpretation possible is as an answer to (5.22),

> (5.22) ¿Quién me llama?
> 'Who is calling me?'

that is, with the agent as the only rhematic element.
The same is true of the following sentences:

> (5.23) a. Los camiones los mandan ELLOS (Naranjo 18).
> 'THEY control the buses.'
>
> b. Eso lo arreglaré yo MISMO (Naranjo 44).
> 'I will take care of that MYSELF.'
>
> c. La casa todavía la pago YO (Naranjo 207).
> 'The house is still being paid for by ME.'

It is clear that these sentences, in contrast with those in (5.13),
answer only questions like (5.24),

> (5.24) a. ¿Quién manda los camiones?
> 'Who controls the buses?'
>
> b. ¿Quién arreglará eso?
> 'Who will take care of that?'
>
> c. ¿Quién paga la casa?
> 'Who is paying for the house?'

not questions like (5.25) or (5.26).

> (5.25) ¿Qué pasa con los camiones (eso, la casa)?
> 'What about the buses (that, the house)?'
>
> (5.26) ¿Qué pasa?
> 'What's up?'

Let us now consider sentences with a cause and a patient, like the
following:

> (5.27) Tu ingenuidad (cause) conmueve hasta las piedras (pat).
> 'Your naïveté moves even rocks.'

With respect to rheme assignment, sentence (5.27) may have either of
the following 'normal' structures:
A) only the patient is rheme;
B) both the patient and the predicate are rhemes;
C) all three constituents are rhemes;
that is, it may answer questions (5.28) (case A), (5.29) (case B), or
(5.30) (case C):

> (5.28) ¿A quién conmueve mi ingenuidad?
> 'Who does my naïveté move?'
>
> (5.29) ¿Qué pasa con mi ingenuidad?
> 'What about my naïveté?'
>
> (5.30) ¿Qué dices?
> 'What are you saying?'

This indicates that the pertinent RSH is as follows:

(5.31) RHEME SELECTION HIERARCHY (TENTATIVE)

    1. Patient

    2. Predicate

    3. Cause

Experiencers and possessors also rank low in the RSH.

Let us consider, for instance, sentences with a patient and a possessor, like the following:

(5.32) a. Necesita usted (poss) unas vacaciones (pat) (Naranjo 66).
      'You need a vacation.'

    b. Tiene usted (poss) los gustos más extraños (pat) (Naranjo 85).
      'You have the strangest tastes.'

These sentences may be interpreted as answers to questions like (5.33),

(5.33) a. ¿Qué necesito?
      'What do I need?'

    b. ¿Qué tengo?
      'What do I have?'

in other words, with the patient as rheme. They can also be interpreted as having both the patient and the predicate as rhemes, that is, as answers to questions like (5.34),

(5.34) ¿Qué dices de mí?
      'What are you saying about me?'

and as consisting entirely of new information, that is, as answers to a question like (5.35).

(5.35) ¿Qué dices?
      'What are you saying?'

This shows that the possessor ranks lowest in the RSH.

Let us now consider some sentences with a patient and an experiencer, like the following:

(5.36) a. Me (exp) cansan tus especulaciones (pat).
      'Your speculations tire me out.'

    b. Ø (exp) he llegado a pensar que estaba en vacaciones (pat) (Naranjo 15).
      'I've come to think that you were on vacation.'

    c. Ø (exp) creía que ya no había hombres en mi tierra (pat) (Vargas Llosa 272).
      'I thought there were no men left in my land.'

    d. Ø (exp) se notaba que era cosa forzada (pat) (Vargas Llosa 274).
      'It was clear that it was an unnatural thing.'

Just as in the previous cases, these sentences allow three different interpretations when the main stress falls on the patient:

A) with a rhematic patient;
B) with predicate and patient as rhemes;
C) with all three constituents as rhemes;

that is, they answer questions like (5.37) (case A), (5.38) (case B), or (5.39) (case C):

(5.37) a. ¿Qué te cansa?
'What tires you out?'

b. ¿Qué ha llegado a pensar usted?
'What have you come to think?'

c. ¿Qué creía usted?
'What did you think?'

d. ¿Qué se notaba?
'What was clear?'

(5.38) ¿Qué dice usted?
'What are you saying?'

(5.39) ¿Qué pasa?
'What's up?'

If, on the other hand, the main stress falls on the experiencer, no other element may be interpreted as rheme. Thus, a sentence like (5.40)

(5.40) Eso lo creía JOSÉ.
'That is what JOSÉ believed.'

answers only question (5.41), not questions (5.42) or (5.43).

(5.41) ¿Quién creía eso?
'Who believed that?'

(5.42) ¿Qué dices de eso?
'What do you say about that?'

(5.43) ¿Qué pasa?
'What's up?'

If we assign the lowest rhematic rank to the experiencer, we also account for the fact that sentences like (5.44),

(5.44) A los borrachos la gente los RESPETA.
'People RESPECT drunks.'

with the main stress on the predicate, allow the experiencer, but not the patient, to be considered as rheme, that is, they answer questions like (5.45) or (5.46), but not questions like (5.47).

(5.45) ¿Qué hace la gente con los borrachos?
'What do people do with drunks?'

(5.46) ¿Qué pasa con los borrachos?
'What about drunks?'

(5.47) ¿Qué pasa?
'What's up?'

We are now in a position to combine the tentative rheme selection hierarchies proposed so far in this chapter. In all of them, the patient ranks highest and the predicate second. They can all be reduced, then, to the following:

(5.48) RHEME SELECTION HIERARCHY (TENTATIVE)

    1. Patient

    2. Predicate

    3. Agent, cause, possessor, experiencer

The rest of the arguments (complement, location, time, source, target, beneficiary and identifier) all rank higher than the patient,[1] which is shown by the following sentences:

(5.49) a. Para escribir una novela hay que ∅ (pat) vivir toda una vi-da (comp) (Naranjo 9).
'In order to write a novel one must live a whole life.'

    b. Mi amigo (pat) vivía en esa casucha (loc).
'My friend lived in that hut.'

    c. La conferencia (pat) es mañana (time).
'The lecture is tomorrow.'

    d. Mi padre (pat) es de Piura (so).
'My father is from Piura.'

    e. Estos camiones (pat) no sirven para nada (targ) (Naranjo 20).
'These buses are good for nothing.'

    f. Las ganancias (pat) son para el patrón (ben).
'The earnings are for the boss.'

    g. Esto (pat) es una estafa organizada (ident) (Naranjo 45).
'This is an organized swindle.'

In fact, all these sentences allow three interpretations:
A) with the rightmost argument as rheme;
B) with the rightmost argument and the predicate as rhemes;
C) with all three constituents as rhemes.
In other words, these sentences answer questions like (5.50) (case A), (5.51) (case B), or (5.52) (case C).

(5.50) a. Para escribir una novela, ¿hay que vivir qué?
'In order to write a novel one must live what?'

    b. ¿Dónde vivía tu amigo?
'Where did your friend live?'

    c. ¿Cuándo es la conferencia?
'When is the lecture?'

    d. ¿De dónde es tu padre?
'Where is your father from?'

    e. ¿Para qué (no) sirven esos camiones?
'What are those buses (not) good for?'

    f. ¿Para quién son las ganancias?
'Who are the earnings for?'

    g. ¿Qué es esto?
'What is this?'

(5.51) a. ¿Qué hay que hacer para escribir una novela?
'What must one do in order to write a novel?'

    b. ¿Qué hay con tu amigo?
       'What about your friend?'

    c. ¿Qué hay con la conferencia?
       'What about the lecture?'

    d. ¿Qué dices de tu padre?
       'What about your father?'

    e. ¿Qué hay con esos camiones?
       'What about those buses?'

    f. ¿Qué hay con las ganancias?
       'What about the earnings?'

    g. ¿Qué hay con esto?
       'What about this?'

(5.52) ¿Qué pasa?
       'What's up?'

The RSH for these cases is, then, the following:

(5.53) RHEME SELECTION HIERARCHY (TENTATIVE)

    1. Complement, location, time, source, target, beneficiary,
       identifier.

    2. Predicate

    3. Patient

Combining it with RSH (5.48), we obtain the following:

(5.54) RHEME SELECTION HIERARCHY (TENTATIVE)

    1. Complement, location, time, source, target, beneficiary,
       identifier

    2. Predicate

    3. Patient

    4. Predicate

    5. Agent, cause, possessor, experiencer

This hierarchy predicts that the predicate will always rank second in
two-argument sentences. It also establishes an order of rheme selection for
sentences without a patient, for instance, (5.55).

(5.55) El espía (ag) caminó hacia las afueras de la ciudad (targ).
       'The spy walked towards the outskirts of the city.'

As predicted by the RSH, the first choice as rheme is the target, then
the predicate, then the agent. In other words, if the target is selected
as rheme, everything else may be interpreted as rheme also; if the highest ranking rheme is the predicate, only the agent can be included in the
rhematic portion of the sentence, and if the agent ranks highest, nothing
else can be interpreted as rhematic. Thus, (5.55) may answer either (5.56),
(5.57), or (5.58).

(5.56) ¿Hacia dónde caminó el espía?
       'Where did the spy walk to?'

(5.57) ¿Qué hizo el espía?
       'What did the spy do?'

(5.58) ¿Qué pasó?
'What happened?'

On the other hand, a sentence like (5.59)

(5.59) El espía CAMINÓ hacia las afueras de la ciudad.
'The spy WALKED towards the outskirts of the city.'

can only answer (5.60) or (5.61),

(5.60) ¿Cómo se fue el espía a las afueras de la ciudad?
'How did the spy go to the outskirts of the city?'

(5.61) ¿Qué dices de las afueras de la ciudad?
'What do you say about the outskirts of the city?'

and a sentence like (5.62)

(5.62) Hacia las afueras de la ciudad caminó el ESPÍA.
'The SPY walked towards the outskirts of the city.'

can only answer a question (5.63).

(5.63) ¿Quién caminó hacia las afueras de la ciudad?
'Who walked towards the outskirts of the city?'

Hierarchy (5.54) constitutes a hypothesis about the relative 'newness' of different notions. It says that complements, location, time, sources, targets, beneficiaries and identifiers are normally either the only or the most prominent piece of new information, that patients come next, and finally agents, causes, possessors and experiencers. It also says that the predicate always ranks second, which accounts for the fact that very often both the predicate and the highest ranking argument constitute new information. The unity thus created between the predicate and a specific argument accounts for the fact that the grammar may treat these two constituents as a higher unit, which has prompted many grammarians to recognize a deep structure constituent known as 'verb phrase' or 'predicate phrase'. In our grammar, such a constituent is unnecessary, however, since the RSH predicts the unity noted without the addition of other kinds of constituents.

5.3 Three-argument sentences

The analysis of three-argument sentences in general confirms the RSH which we have established for two-argument sentences. Two modifications, however, appear to be necessary:
a) Since the rank of the predicate would be ambiguous for a sentence with three arguments (it may be either second or fourth), we exclude it from the RSH and specify its rhematic rank by means of a special rule:

(5.64) The predicate always ranks one step higher than the lowest
        ranking argument.

b) Since sentences with three arguments may include an instrument as the highest ranking element, we must add this argument to the RSH.
With these modifications, we obtain the following revised version of the RSH:

(5.65) RHEME SELECTION HIERARCHY (TENTATIVE)

1. Complement, location, time, source, target, beneficiary, identifier, instrument

2. Patient

3. Agent, cause, possessor, experiencer

Let us examine now some sentences with three arguments:

(5.66) a. Usté, que poco conoce a los hombres (ag), le llamará a eso (pat) sabe Dios qué (comp) (Arguedas II.118).
'You, who know men badly, will call that God knows what.'

b. Don Fermín (ag) sacó sus espuelas (pat) de la sala (so) (Arguedas II.20).
'Don Fermín took his spurs from the room.'

c. El director (ag) pidió este equipo (pat) por teléfono (inst).
'The director ordered this equipment by phone.'

d. Ese porcentaje (cause) lo convierte a usted (pat), de todos modos, en millonario (targ) (Arguedas II.76).
'That percentage makes you, anyway, a millionaire.'

e. El jefe (poss) tiene la mente (pat) en blanco (comp).
'The boss's mind is blank.'

f. Ø (poss) tuve tres hormigas (pat) en una caja de fósforos (loc) (Naranjo 187).
'I had three ants in a match box.'

g. La colonia (exp) sólo quería al hombre (pat) de rodillas (comp) (Arguedas II.11).
'The colony only wanted man on his knees.'

h. Para mí (exp) lo que usted me dice (pat) son puros cuentos (ident) (Naranjo 44).
'To me, what you tell me is all baloney.'

We see that the agent (a-c), the cause (d), the possessor (e, f), or the experiencer (g, h) rank lowest, then the predicate, the patient and the remaining argument, in that order.

All these sentences show considerable contextual freedom. Thus, for instance, sentence (5.66g) may answer any of the following questions:

(5.67) a. ¿Cómo quería la colonia al hombre?
'How did the colony want man?'
(rhematic complement)

b. ¿Qué quería la colonia?
'What did the colony want?'
(rhematic patient and complement)

c. ¿Qué pasaba con la colonia?
'What about the colony?'
(rhematic predicate, patient and complement)

d. ¿Qué sucedía?
'What was happening?'
(all four constituents are rhematic)

On the other hand, if the RSH is violated, as in (5.68),

(5.68) La colonia quería de rodillas al HOMBRE.
'The colony wanted MAN on his knees.'

the sentence can only answer a question like (5.69).

(5.69) ¿A quién quería de rodillas la colonia?
'Who did the colony want on his knees?'

As these examples show, the RSH postulated predicts accurately the rhematic behavior of three-argument sentences.

5.4 Four-argument sentences

The analysis of four-argument sentences suggests that among the highest ranking arguments, the instrument and the target rank higher than the rest. Consider, for instance, the following sentences:

(5.70) a. Juan (ag) le compró un anillo (pat) a María (ben) con unos ahorros (inst).
'John bought Mary a ring with some savings.'

b. Juan (ag) le compró un anillo (pat) a María (ben) para conquistarla (targ).
'John bought Mary a ring in order to woo her.'

which behave 'normally' with respect to rheme assignment, that is, they allow interpretations which vary in the extension of the rheme, starting from the last constituent. Sentence (5.70a), for instance, answers all of the following questions:

(5.71) a. ¿Con qué le compró un anillo Juan a María?
'What did John buy a ring for Mary with?'
(rhematic instrument)

b. ¿Para quién y con qué compró Juan un anillo?
'For whom and with what did John buy a ring?'
(rhematic instrument and beneficiary)

c. ¿Qué compró Juan, para quién y con qué?
'What did John buy for whom and with what?'
(rhematic instrument, beneficiary and patient)

d. ¿Qué hizo Juan?
'What did John do?'
(rhematic instrument, beneficiary, patient and predicate)

e. ¿Qué pasó?
'What happened?'
(all five constituents are rhematic)

On the other hand, a version that alters this order, like (5.72),

(5.72) A María Juan le compró un anillo con unos ahorros.
'For Mary John bought a ring with some savings.'

cannot answer the same broad range of questions.

On the basis of these examples, it would seem appropriate to modify the RSH in such a way as to reflect this privileged position of instrument and target. I, therefore, suggest this revised version of the RSH:

(5.73) RHEME SELECTION HIERARCHY (TENTATIVE)

    1. Instrument, target

    2. Complement, source, location, time, beneficiary, identifier

    3. Patient

    4. Agent, cause, possessor, experiencer

This hierarchy may need further refinement, but it is more probable that rhematic priority in the rare cases of sentences with more than four arguments is determined by other factors. Thus, the fact that (5.74) is more acceptable than (5.75)

    (5.74) Juan (ag) le compró un anillo (pat) a María (ben) con unos ahorros (inst) para CONQUISTARLA (targ).
        'John bought Mary a ring with some savings in order to WOO her.'

    (5.75) Juan le compró un anillo a María para conquistarla con unos AHORROS.
        'John bought Mary a ring in order to woo her with some SAVINGS.'

seems to depend more on the potential ambiguity of (5.75) -- the phrase para conquistarla con unos ahorros may be interpreted as one or two constituents -- than on a rhematic hierarchical difference between an instrument and a target.

FOOTNOTES TO CHAPTER FIVE

[1]We will consider the instrument when we discuss sentences with three or more constituents.

Chapter Six

SPECIAL CASES

The rheme selection hierarchy established in the preceding chapter
may be altered by certain factors, such as idiomatic expressions, the
presence of a passive marker, of a 'presentational' verb, or of negation.

6.1 Idiomatic expressions

As for the first factor, if an argument forms an idiomatic expression
with the predicate, it may take on a lower rank in the RSH than it would
have otherwise.

For instance, in the following sentences, the predicate and the complement constitute an idiomatic expression, and as a consequence, the complement -- contrary to the norm -- ranks lower than the patient:

(6.1) a. Me contaron que te habían ascendido y que ahora tenés a tu
cargo (comp) la proveeduría y almacenes (pat) (Naranjo 25).
'They told me you had been promoted and now you are in charge
of supplies and stores.'

b. He estado todos estos días poniendo al día (comp) el regis-
tro de circulares (pat) (Naranjo 36).
'All these days I have been bringing the registry of cir-
culars up to date.'

Much more will have to be learned about the behavior of idioms before
these observations can be incorporated formally within our theory.

6.2 Passive sentences

As for passive sentences, it must be observed that the patient takes
on the lowest rhematic rank, while the argument which would normally be
lowest (agent, cause, possessor or experiencer) adopts the rank that would
normally be assigned to the patient.

Assuming that 'passivity' is an inflectional feature of certain verbs,
the alteration which it causes in the RSH may be formulated like this:

(6.2) If the predicate has the feature [+passive], the patient interchanges rank with the agent, cause, possessor or experiencer.

This rule explains that a sentence like the following

(6.3) Víctor Jara fue asesinado por los MILITARES.
'Victor Jara was murdered by the MILITARY.'

allows the following three interpretations:
A) with only the agent as rheme;
B) with the agent and the predicate as rhemes;
C) with all three constituents as rhemes;
while sentence (6.4)

(6.4) Por los militares fue asesinado Víctor JARA.
'Victor JARA was murdered by the military.'

allows only the interpretation where the patient is rheme.
This rule, in conjunction with rule (5.64), which assigns to the

predicate the second lowest rank, also accounts for the fact that sentence
(6.5) allows two interpretations,

(6.5) Víctor Jara fue ASESINADO.
'Victor Jara was MURDERED.'

one with the predicate as rheme, and one where both constituents are rhematic, whereas sentence (6.6) allows only one, with the patient as rheme.

(6.6) Fue asesinado Víctor JARA.
'Victor JARA was murdered.'

The arguments which are not mentioned in rule (6.2) (complement, location, instrument, etc) do not seem to be affected by the presence of a
passive predicate. Thus, for instance, in a sentence like (6.7),

(6.7) El crimen fue consumado por los verdugos en el ESTADIO.
'The crime was consumated by the executioners in the STADIUM.'

the locative phrase en el estadio clearly ranks the highest, just as in
the case of active sentences, since (6.7) has greater contextual freedom
than, say, (6.8).

(6.8) El crimen fue consumado en el estadio por los VERDUGOS.
'The crime was consumated in the stadium by the EXECUTIONERS.'

6.3 Presentational verbs

Let us now consider the effect of 'presentational' verbs on the RSH.
The latest version of the RSH, let us recall, is as follows:

(5.73) RHEME SELECTION HIERARCHY (TENTATIVE)

1. Instrument, target

2. Complement, location, time, source, beneficiary, identifier

3. Patient

4. Agent, cause, possessor, experiencer

Let us also recall the special rule posited for the rhematic status
of the predicate:

(5.64) The predicate always ranks one step higher than the lowest
ranking argument.

One of the predictions made by the RSH and the special predicate rule
is that in a sentence consisting only of a patient and a predicate, the
latter ranks higher than the former. This prediction is borne out by sentences like (6.9),

(6.9) El canario MURIÓ.
'The canary DIED.'

which has greater contextual freedom than (6.10),

(6.10) Murió el CANARIO.
'The CANARY died.'

since it answers either (6.11) or (6.12),

(6.11) ¿Qué pasó con el canario?
'What happened to the canary?'

(6.12) ¿Qué pasó?
'What happened?'

while (6.10) answers only (6.13).

(6.13) ¿Quién murió?
'Who died?'

However, the prediction fails in the case of a sentence like (6.14),

(6.14) La resistencia EMPEZÓ.
'The resistance STARTED.'

since, as we have seen, this sentence is more restricted contextually than (6.15).

(6.15) Empezó la RESISTENCIA.
'The RESISTANCE started.'

In fact, when we discussed this sentence type at the beginning of the preceding chapter, we established a tentative RSH (5.11), which contradicts rule (5.64):

(5.11) RHEME SELECTION HIERARCHY (TENTATIVE)

1. Patient

2. Predicate denoting 'beginning', 'existence', 'appearance', etc.

This contradiction must, of course, be resolved.

The predicates mentioned by RSH (5.11) have been extensively studied by Hatcher (1956), who divides them into categories like the following:

a) Existence - presence
...desde sus dolientes muros donde vive la hiedra (Cela 1952:25)/
...las montañas, en cuyos hondones húmedos todavía habitaba la no-che (Miró 202) / Sólo con aceite; pero que abunde el pan (Clarasó 115).

b) Absence
...Falta dirección, sobra gente (Pérez Galdós 20) / Aún faltan veinte minutos (Sainz de Robles 105).

c) Beginning
Entonces empezará el año (Díaz Cañabate 205) /... Los paisanos se retraen a sus casas. Comienza el invierno (Palacio Valdés 173) / Qué se le va a hacer; empiezan los sustos (Díaz Cañabate 107).

d) Continuing - remaining
¡Cierto como hay Dios...Sigue la bola! ¡Ahora Villa contra Carran-za (Azuela 105) / Pero no pueden continuar nuestras relaciones (U-namuno 80) / No queda otro recurso que beber (Benavente 36).

e) Production
Pisa usté y nasen flores (Alvarez Quintero 258) / Pasó un mes, y ...no brotó nada de lo plantado por él (Pío Baroja 114) / Y en la casa se restablecieron las antiguas costumbres y reinó el habitual desorden (Pío Baroja 90).

f) Occurrence
Supongo que no habrán ocurrido desgracias (Hartzenbusch 22) / En el verano no pueden pasar más que desastres (Alvarez Quintero 210) / El hombre es fuego y la mujer estopa, y luego, pues pasan las cosas (Cela 1951:45).

g) Appearing

Algunas rezagadas llegaban...Aparecieron cubiertos, platos (Villarta 87) / ...porque al trasladarse de domicilio aparecen los objetos perdidos (Medio 126) / Miró. Del bolsillo del policía asomaban los plateados flejes de las esposas (Cela 1951:110).

h) Coming

¡Qué noche más hermosa! Viene un olor a jazmines (Martínez Sierra 11) / No crea esa señora que a los pueblos no llega la moda (Arniches y Barrera 53) / ...pero creo que se avecinan días no muy pacíficos (Medio 272).

The feature which is common to all these sentences, as Hatcher perceptively noted, is that their function is to introduce the patient, to present it, so to say, to the addressee's consciousness.

Let us say, then, that the verbs illustrated in the preceding examples have the feature [+presentational]. This allows us to replace the tentative RSH (5.11) and the predicate rule (5.64) by the following special rule:

(6.16) The predicate always ranks one step higher than the lowest ranking argument, except when the predicate is [+presentational], in which case its rank is lower than that of the predicate.

It must be observed that, with a few exceptions like <u>haber</u> 'there to be, to exist', <u>suceder</u>, <u>ocurrir</u>, <u>pasar</u> 'to happen', the verbs studied by Hatcher may or may not be presentational. Thus, for instance, the verb <u>entrar</u> 'to come in' is presentational in sentence (6.17) but not in sentence (6.18).

(6.17) En ese momento, entró un SOLDADO.
       'At that moment, a SOLDIER came in.'

(6.18) Valientemente, el soldado ENTRÓ.
       'Bravely, the soldier came IN.'

This indicates that for most of these verbs the feature [+presentational] is an inflectional feature assigned optionally by a lexical redundancy rule like the following:

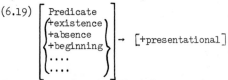

$$(6.19) \begin{bmatrix} \text{Predicate} \\ \begin{cases} \text{+existence} \\ \text{+absence} \\ \text{+beginning} \\ \dots \\ \dots \end{cases} \end{bmatrix} \rightarrow [\text{+presentational}]$$

In the case of verbs like <u>haber</u>, <u>suceder</u>, etc., on the other hand, this feature is presumably specified in the lexicon as an inherent feature.

Notice, furthermore, that the underlying category of the argument which co-occurs with a presentational verb may vary when this verb is used non-presentationally. Thus, for instance, in sentence (6.17), <u>un soldado</u> must be considered a patient, whereas in (6.18) <u>el soldado</u> is an agent. This difference is reflected, for instance, in the fact that an adverb like <u>valientemente</u> 'bravely' is compatible with sentence (6.18) but not with (6.17).

Besides presentational verbs which co-occur only with a patient, there are some that may also take a location or a source, as in the following sentences:

(6.20) a. Pues detrasito de ella (loc) está la Media Luna (pat) (Rulfo 11).
'Right behind her is the Half Moon.'

b. Vayan a Huancabamba, Ayabaca, Chulucanas, de todas partes
(so) salen cholas orgullosas de haber dormido con mi tío
Chápiro (pat) (Vargas Llosa 274).
'Go to Huancabamba, Ayabaca, Chulucanas, from everywhere
there come cholas who are proud to have slept with my uncle
Chápiro.'

In these cases, the rhematic hierarchy is different from what it
would be with a non-presentational verb, since it is the patient, not the
other argument, that has the rhematic priority. Since rule (6.16) speci-
fies the rhematic rank of the patient only with respect to the presentational predicate, and not with respect to the other argument, another rule
is needed to accomplish this, like the following:

(6.21) If the verb has the feature [+presentational], the patient
interchanges its rhematic rank with that of the other argument present.

The parallelism between this rule and the one that alters the rhematic hierarchy in sentences with passive verbs, namely (6.2), suggests
an unsuspected relationship between the features presentational and passive. From a rhematic point of view, both features serve to give prominence to an argument which ordinarily would not have it, the patient in
the case of the feature presentational, and the agent, the cause, the possessor or the experiencer in the case of the feature passive.

6.4 The role of negation

Finally, let us consider the influence of negation on the rhematic
hierarchy.

Notice, to begin with, that negation raises the rhematic rank of the
constituent it affects. Thus, for instance, in contrast with the greater
contextual freedom of (6.22) with respect to (6.23),

(6.22) Salió el SOL.
'The SUN came out.'

(6.23) El sol SALIÓ.
'The sun came OUT.'

we observe that the presence of negation reverses this state of affairs,
giving the predicate a higher rhematic rank than that of the patient:
(6.24) has greater contextual freedom than (6.25).

(6.24) El sol no SALIÓ.
'The sun didn't come OUT.'

(6.25) No salió el SOL.
'The SUN didn't come out.'

Notice, furthermore, that negation may affect different sentence constituents. Thus, for instance, in the following sentences, it affects the
agent, the predicate, and the patient respectively:

(6.26) a. Esa casa no la construyó PEDRO.
'PETER didn't build that house.'

> b. Esa casa Pedro no la CONSTRUYÓ.
>   'Peter didn't BUILD that house.'

> c. Pedro no construyó esa CASA.
>   'Peter didn't build that HOUSE.'

Negation may also affect more than one constituent, provided the rhematic hierarchy is not violated. Sentence (6.26c), which follows the rhematic hierarchy allows, besides the interpretation indicated, one where the predicate and the patient are negated, and another where the whole sentence is negated. In other words, this sentence may be followed by any of these:

> (6.27) a. ...construyó un hospital.
>   'he built a hospital.'

>   b. ...se fue de vacaciones.
>   'he went on vacation.'

>   c. ...Pablo no escribió esa novela: nadie hizo nada.
>   'Paul didn't write that novel: nobody did anything.'

On the other hand, sentences (6.26a) and (6.26b), which violate the rhematic hierarchy, allow just the interpretations suggested, where only one constituent is negated. Thus, it is possible to complete sentence (6.26a) with (6.28a), but not with (6.28b) or (6.28c).

> (6.28) a. La construyó JUAN.
>   'JOHN built it.'

>   b. Juan la DESTRUYÓ.
>   'John DESTROYED it.'

>   c. Nadie hizo nada ese verano.
>   'Nobody did anything that summer.'

By the same token, sentence (6.26b) may only be followed by (6.29a) not by (6.29b) or (6.29c).

> (6.29) a. La PLANEÓ.
>   'He PLANNED it.'

>   b. Esa casa la planeó JUAN.
>   'JOHN planned that house.'

>   c. Nadie hizo nada ese verano.
>   'Nobody did anything that summer.'

This indicates that negative, as well as affirmative, sentences are subject to the rheme selection hierarchy. The presence of a negation, however, raises the rhematic rank of the constituent which is being negated, as shown by sentences (6.22) through (6.25).

In the absence of a deeper study of the properties of negative sentences, it is not possible to state the relevant rules more precisely. Let us notice, however, by way of conclusion, that a negated constituent, in spite of its high rhematic rank, does not always function as a rheme. Thus, for instance, sentence (6.30) allows two interpretations,

> (6.30) No salió el SOL.
>   'The SUN didn't come out.'

one as in (6.31), where the negated constituent is rhematic,

> (6.31) Lo que salió no fue el SOL (fue la luna).
>   'What came out was not the SUN (it was the moon).'

and another, as in (6.32), where the negated constituent is thematic.

(6.32) Lo que no salió fue el SOL.
'What didn't come out was the SUN.'

6.5 Conclusions

We have shown that the rhematic hierarchy is altered by factors like idiomatic expressions, the presence of a passive or presentational verb, and the presence of negation.

All of these cases require special rules the precise formulation of which is not always clear, given our ignorance with respect to most of these phenomena.

It is interesting, however, that a rhematic approach reveals an unsuspected parallelism between the features passive and presentational, both of which give prominence to an argument which would otherwise rank low in the rhematic hierarchy.

Chapter Seven

ADJUNCTS

This chapter will deal with the rhematic properties of the constituents which we have called adjuncts, which correspond for the most part to traditional adverbs and conjunctions.

Some adverbial expressions have already been dealt with, since they function as arguments, for instance, those in (7.1) and (7.2).

(7.1) La United Brands todavía compra presidentes <u>con dólares</u> (inst).
'United Brands still buys presidents with dollars.'

(7.2) López Arellano vive <u>en España</u> (loc).
'López Arellano lives in Spain.'

We will have nothing more to say about these in their capacity of arguments. However, since locative expressions may also function as adjuncts, as in (7.3),

(7.3) En España, Oswaldo vivirá a cuerpo de rey.
'In Spain, Oswaldo will live like a king.'

they will be dealt with as such in this chapter.

7.1 Different types of adjuncts

From the point of view of their relationship to the rest of the sentence, we may distinguish two kinds of adjuncts: a) immediate constituents of the sentence; b) mediate constituents of the sentence, i.e. constituents of constituents.

The following are examples of a):

(7.4) a. <u>Francamente</u>, no podría dedicarme a este trabajo con la idea de que algo anda mal (33).[1]
'Frankly, I couldn't devote myself to this job with the idea that something was wrong.'

b. <u>Por lo menos</u> no lo hacen en media calle (105).
'At least they don't do it in the middle of the street.'

c. <u>A veces</u> pienso que la gente debía pedir permiso para hablar... (60).
'Sometimes I think people ought to ask permission to speak..'

d. Somos una voz activa <u>todo el tiempo</u> (60).
'We are an active voice all the time.'

Mediate constituents of the sentence are illustrated by the following examples:

(7.5) a. Un abandono que se ve <u>hasta</u> en los escritorios...(33).
'A neglect which you see even on the desks...'

b. Yo <u>sólo</u> he hecho lo que hacen muchos (105).
'I have only done what many people do.'

c. <u>Precisamente</u> eso te pasa en el trabajo (98).
'It is precisely that what happens to you at work.'

    d. Estás <u>apenas</u> empezando a saber lo que es la vida (107).
       'You are just beginning to learn what life is.'

Some adjuncts may function in both capacities, for instance, <u>prácticamente</u> 'practically', which is an immediate constituent of the sentence in (7.6) but a constituent of the identifier in (7.7).

    (7.6) <u>Prácticamente</u> te veía en todos los rostros de mujer...(175).
         'Practically I would see you in every woman's face...'

    (7.7) Recordá que Quesada era <u>prácticamente</u> un hombre feliz...(123).
         'Remember that Quesada was practically a happy man...'

From the viewpoint of rhematic function, only adjuncts which are constituents of the sentence may be assigned the feature [+rheme].

7.2 Non-rhematic adjuncts

Not all adjuncts which are major sentence constituents may function as rhemes. Specifically, there is a class of adjuncts which fall outside the propositional content of the sentence (for a definition of this concept, see Langacker 1974:645ff, who however prefers the expression <u>objective content</u>). They comprise the following subclasses: a) attitude indicators; b) sentence relators; c) topical adjuncts; and d) rhematizers.

    Class a), as the name indicates, includes adjuncts which indicate the speaker's attitude with respect to the message contained in the sentence. Their linear order is quite free, as shown by the following examples:

    (7.8) a. Será un excelente compañero y <u>francamente</u> me sentiré honrado
          de colaborar con él (59).
          'He will be an excellent partner and <u>frankly</u> I will be honor
          ed to collaborate with him.'

        b. Te felicito por tu nombramiento, muy merecido <u>por cierto</u>
          (43).
          'I congratulate you on your appointment, <u>certainly</u> well de
          served.'

        c. Si estuviera en tu lugar, aprovecharía las cosas buenas que
          <u>sin duda</u> tenés (62).
          'If I were in your place, I would take advantage of the good
          things which you undoubtedly have.'

        d. Mire: <u>con franqueza</u> no le entiendo nada (133).
          'Look: frankly I don't understand a thing you say.'

Examples of adjuncts of class b) are the following:

    (7.9) a. Ya existe un dicho clásico: mal de muchos, consuelo de ton
          tos. <u>Así es que</u> debés pensar en vos mismo, en tu propia res
          ponsabilidad (106).
          'There is a classical saying: the sorrow of many is fools'
          consolation. So you must think of yourself, of your own res
          ponsibility.'

        b. Nadie ha chistado. <u>En todo caso</u>, si llegaran a reclamar algo,
          saben bien que tendría que tomar medidas enérgicas (35).
          'Nobody has complained. At any rate, if they did, they know
          very well that I would have to take drastic measures.'

    c. Que lo hagan. <u>Al fin y al cabo</u>, eso es lo que quieren esos
       mierdas (51).
       'Let them do it. After all, that is what those shitheads
       want.'

    d. Dejate de lloriqueos, que los hombres no lloran. <u>Por lo me-</u>
       <u>nos</u> no lo hacen en media calle (105).
       'Stop whimpering; men don't cry. <u>At least</u>, they don't do it
       in the middle of the street.'

    The third class of adjuncts which are normally not rhematic has been
labelled 'topical'. They all show the adverb-forming suffix -<u>mente</u> '-ly',
but differ both in semantic interpretation and in rhematic possibilities
from regular manner adverbs. These adjuncts are normally paraphrasable as
<u>Xmente hablando</u> 'Xly speaking' or <u>hablando en términos X</u> 'speaking in X
terms', and they serve to announce the context within which the sentence
is to be interpreted, hence the label topical. These adjuncts normally occur in initial position. A couple of examples follows:

    (7.10) a. <u>Técnicamente</u>, el problema no tiene solución.
          'Technically, the problem has no solution.'

       b. <u>Estructuralmente</u>, no hay idiomas primitivos.
         'Structurally, there are no primitive languages.'

    A fourth class of sentence adjuncts which are ineligible for rhematic
status consists of adjuncts whose function seems to be that of 'rhematizers', i.e. adjuncts which indicate the rhematic status of other constituents. Some examples follow:

    (7.11) a. <u>Sólo</u> estaba tratando de entretener al señor Quesada mien-
          tras usted venía (54).
          'I was just trying to entertain Mr. Quesada before you
          came.'

       b. <u>Hasta</u> se ha atrevido a decirme que tiene unas cuantas in-
         quietudes con respecto a mi trabajo (61).
         'He has even dared to tell me that he has some doubts with
         respect to my job.'

       c. <u>Simplemente</u> a mí no me importará (60).
         'It will just not matter to me.'

    It is easy to see that these sentences can only be interpreted as
consisting entirely of new information (with the exception of the rhematizer), and that fact is obviously related to the presence of the sentence-initial adjuncts, since without them the sentences would be interpreted as either consisting entirely of new information or as consisting
only partly of new information.

    It appears that all the adjuncts in this class can also mark only
part of the sentence as rhematic, for instance, <u>hasta</u> 'even' in the following sentence,

    (7.12) Ya debe saber <u>hasta</u> la fecha de nacimiento del último pariente
       de Quesada (144).
       'By now you must even now the birth date of Quesada's last
       relative.'

which only signals the patient as rhematic; consequently we will deal with
rhematizers as a unified class after we discuss the rest of the adjuncts

which are immediate constituents of the sentence.

7.3 Potentially rhematic adjuncts

We are now ready to discuss those adjuncts which are potential rhemes. They include manner, time and locative adverbs, as shown by the following examples:

(7.13) a. La gente que pasaba a mi lado, podría juzgarme por mi ves-
           tido y quizás verme un poco despectivamente (137).
           'The people walking by me could judge me by my dress and
           look at me a little disparagingly.'

       b. ...le ruego que el proyecto de respuesta esté dentro de una
          hora (34).
          '...I ask you to have the draft of the response ready with-
          in an hour.'

       c. Voy a aceptar tu consejo y me voy a sentar en una banca del
          parque...(57)
          'I'll take your advice and I'll sit on a park bench.'

In terms of the system of rules proposed in chapters five through nine, these adjuncts may be assigned the feature [+rheme] freely. However, just as in the case of arguments, their place in the RSH must be determined so that the linear order rules may apply to them.
We have seen in the previous chapters that sentences where the poten- tial rhemes appear in an ascending hierarchical order from left to right are characterized by a great degree of freedom as far as rhematic struc- ture goes, that is, they can consist entirely of rhematic material, or one or more constituents starting from the left can be presented as old in- formation. With this in mind, let us examine the following sentences, all of which contain a manner adverbial in final position:

(7.14) a. Le ruego prepararme un proyecto de respuesta en forma in-
           mediata (32).
           'I'm asking you to prepare a draft for a reply at once.'

       b. Le ruego no coger eso literalmente (149).
          'I beg you not to take that literally.'

       c. Esta carta la contestaré personalmente (153).
          'This letter I will answer personally.'

       d. Coja las cosas con calma...(116)
          'Take things calmly...'

In all of these cases, the relevant clause contains an agent, a pre- dicate, a patient and a manner adverbial. It is easily seen that the latter ranks highest for the purposes of rheme selection. For instance, (7.14c) may answer either (7.15) or (7.16),

(7.15) ¿Cómo contestarás esta carta?
       'How will you answer this letter?'

(7.16) ¿Qué harás con esta carta?
       'What will you do with this letter?'

whereas (7.17) can only answer the (improbable) question (7.18).

(7.17) Esta carta personalmente la CONTESTARÉ.
       'This letter I will ANSWER personally.'

(7.18) ¿Qué harás personalmente con esta carta?
'What will you do with this letter personally?'

Another indication that manner adverbials rank higher than the other
constituents in the sentences under consideration comes from the fact that
while a sentence like (7.19)

(7.19) Contestaré esta carta PERSONALMENTE.
'I'll answer this letter PERSONALLY.'

may answer any of the questions in (7.20),

(7.20) a. ¿Cómo contestarás esta carta?
'How will you answer this letter?'

b. ¿Qué contestarás y cómo?
'What will you answer and how?'

c. ¿Qué harás?
'What will you do?'

a sentence like (7.21) may only answer a question like (7.22).

(7.21) Contestaré personalmente esta CARTA.
'I'll answer this LETTER personally.'

(7.22) ¿Qué contestarás personalmente?
'What will you answer personally?'

Having demonstrated that manner adverbials rank higher than agents,
predicates and patients for rheme selection purposes, we must still determine their place with respect to high ranking arguments like instrument,
target, complement, source, location, time, identifier and beneficiary.
Since, according to RSH (5.73), instrument and target rank higher than the
rest, it will be enough to show how manner adverbials rank with respect to
these to establish also their place with respect to the other arguments.
A sentence like (7.23)

(7.23) No tuve oportunidad de conversar con los doctores directamente
(145).
'I didn't have the chance to talk with the doctors directly.'

shows that the manner adverbial ranks higher than the target con los doctores 'with the doctors', since it allows a wider variety of rhematic interpretations than a version with the target at the end and carrying the
main sentential stress.
As for their place with respect to instruments, manner adverbials
seem to rank at the same level with them. Thus both of the following sentences seem to have comparable rhematic possibilities:

(7.24) a. Cerré la puerta con llave CUIDADOSAMENTE.
'I locked the door CAREFULLY.'

b. Cerré la puerta cuidadosamente con LLAVE.
'I carefully LOCKED the door.'

This suggests the following revised version of the RSH:

(7.25) RHEME SELECTION HIERARCHY (TENTATIVE)

    1. Instrument, manner adverbial

    2. Target

    3. Complement, source, location, time, identifier, beneficiary

    4. Patient

    5. Agent, cause, possessor, experiencer

For convenience, I will refer to high ranking adverbials -- restricted to manner adverbials so far, but to be extended to other kinds later -- as strong. Contrasting with these, some adverbials are weak, in the sense that they tend to occur in the non-rhematic portion of the sentence. These include for the most part some time adverbials like hoy 'today', a veces 'sometimes', ahora 'now', últimamente 'lately', etc., and some place adverbials like en Europa 'in Europe', en América Latina 'in Latin America', etc. The following examples illustrate weak time adverbials:

(7.26) a. Hoy, desde que leí el periódico, no he tenido tranquilidad (35).
'Today, since I read the newspaper, I have had no peace of mind.'

    b. A veces pienso que la gente debía pedir permiso para hablar (60).
'Sometimes I think people ought to ask permission to talk.'

    c. Al principio creí que era usted sólo un oficinista...(134)
'At first I thought you were just an office worker...'

    d. Ahora entramos al campo de lo relativo (113).
'Now we enter the field of the relative.'

In order to sustantiate the claim that these adjuncts are weak, that is, they rank lower than anything else in the sentence, consider, for instance, the last sentence, which can answer any of the questions in (7.27),

(7.27) a. ¿Dónde entramos ahora?
'What do we enter now?'

    b. ¿Qué pasa ahora?
'What happens now?'

    c. ¿Qué pasa?
'What's up?'

and compare it with (7.28),

(7.28) Entramos al campo de lo relativo AHORA.
'We enter the field of the relative NOW.'

which can only answer (7.29).

(7.29) ¿Cuándo entramos al campo de lo relativo?
'When do we enter the field of the relative?'

For our rules to assign the order shown by (7.26d) when all constituents are rhematic, i.e. when the sentence answers question (7.27c), the adjunct ahora 'now' must rank lower than anything else in the sentence. Similarly, for the adjunct ahora to be assigned final position and the main sentential stress as in (7.28), everything else must be non-rhematic, which is in fact the case with this sentence.

From the point of view of communication, 'weak' adjuncts like ahora 'now', a veces 'sometimes', al principio 'at first' serve primarily to provide a time reference for the most 'informative' part of the sentence. Consequently, their selection as rhemes over other constituents, as in (7.28), is atypical.

But not all time adverbials are weak. Those illustrated in the following sentences, for instance, would seem to rank as high as manner adverbials:

(7.30) a. Reúna todos los datos que pueda a la mayor brevedad (32).
'Gather all the information you can as soon as possible.'

b. Con estos calores es siempre molesto viajar en autobús (92).
'In this heat, it is always uncomfortable to travel by bus.'

c. Considero que se trata de una campaña y hay que pararla de inmediato (32).
'I think it is a campaign and it must be stopped immediately.'

These adverbials seem to carry an intrinsic informational load higher than that of adverbials like hoy 'today', ahora 'now', etc., which in order to function as rhemes must often be strengthened as in the expressions hoy mismo 'this very day', ahora mismo 'right now.'

A similar dichotomy seems to apply to place adverbials. On the one hand, as we have already indicated, expressions with a 'general' meaning like en Europa 'in Europe', en América Latina 'in Latin America', etc. seem to occur primarily in the non-rhematic portion of the sentence and have as main function that of providing a 'location' for the more informative part of the sentence; on the other, more specific expressions like en medio del río 'in the middle of the river', encima del mostrador 'on top of the counter', tend to outrank other constituents as potential rhemes.

On the basis of these observations, I offer the following revised version of the RSH:

(7.31) RHEME SELECTION HIERARCHY

1. Instrument, manner adverbial, 'strong' time and place adverbial

2. Target

3. Complement, source, location, time, identifier, beneficiary

4. Patient

5. Agent, cause, possessor, experiencer

6. 'Weak' time and place adverbial

The dividing line between strong and weak adverbials is by no means clear, however. Since the distinction seems to correlate with degree of generality, a gradient, rather than a clear-cut dichotomy, is to be expected. In view of this fact, it is hard to formalize the behavior of these adjuncts. I will simply suggest, then, that the lexical specification of adjuncts includes features indicating whether they may or may not undergo the rule of RHEME ASSIGNMENT, and for those that may, what rank they have in the RSH, leaving unsolved the problem posed by the lack of a clear-cut dividing line between strong and weak adjuncts.

7.4 Mediate sentence constituents

We now turn to adjuncts which are not immediate constituents of the
sentence. The following examples illustrate this type of adjunct:

(7.32) a. Estás <u>totalmente</u> equivocado (113).
        'You're completely wrong.'

       b. <u>Hasta</u> los jefes se van en punto...(36)
        'Even bosses leave right on time...'

       c. Quiero <u>simplemente</u> descansar (100).
        'I just want to rest.'

       d. Yo sólo he hecho lo que hacen muchos (105).
        'I've only done what many people do.'

We must distinguish two sub-classes among these adjuncts: 'rhematizers', illustrated in (7.32b-d), and the sub-class illustrated by <u>completa-</u>
<u>mente</u> in (7.32a). We will concern ourselves only with the former.
   Given the fact that this study is restricted to the rhematic organiza-
tion and linear order of major sentence constituents, we should exclude all
adjuncts which are not immediate constituents of the sentence from consideration. However, the class of rhematizers is crucially related to the
central topic of this book, and we must consequently deal with it.
   Earlier in this chapter, we discussed rhematizers which affect the
whole sentence, and indicated that apparently all the adjuncts in that
class may also be used to mark only part of the sentence as rhematic. This
is certainly true at least of the following adjuncts: <u>apenas</u> 'just', <u>casi</u>
'almost', <u>hasta</u> 'even', <u>ni siquiera</u> 'not even', <u>prácticamente</u> 'practically', <u>precisamente</u> 'precisely', <u>simplemente</u> 'simply', <u>solamente</u>, <u>sólo</u> 'only' and <u>ya</u> 'already', as shown by the following examples, where the adjunct marks the whole sentence as rhematic in the a-sentences, and only
part of it in the b-sentences:

(7.33) a. (--¿Leyó usted los periódicos?)
          --<u>Apenas</u> he tenido tiempo de hojearlos (32).
          '(Did you read the newspapers?)
          I have just had enough time to glance at them.'

       b. (Yo ya no soy nada.) Soy <u>apenas</u> la protección que doy a mi
          familia (55).
          '(I'm no longer anything.) I'm just the protection which I
          give my family.'

(7.34) a. Cuando se iba por la calle con él, <u>casi</u> había que correr
          (123).
          'When you walked on the street with him, you almost had to
          run.'

       b. Es <u>casi</u> un niño.
          'He's almost a child.'

(7.35) a. ...tengo detrás de mí una leyenda un poco negra. <u>Hasta</u> me
          llaman terciopelo, por lo peligroso que siempre me han en-
          contrado (61).
          '...I have a somewhat black legend behind me. They even call
          me velvet, that's how dangerous they've always considered
          me.'

      b. Lo tengo para todo, <u>hasta</u> para dejar mandados (94).
         'I use it for everything, even to run errands.'

(7.36) a. ...<u>ni siquiera</u> había espacio dónde poner su escritorio (60).
         'There wasn't even room for his desk.'

      b. El hablar así me demuestra que no tenés <u>ni siquiera</u> una i-
         dea de lo que se tiene que aguantar en un trabajo...(98)
         'Your speaking like that shows me that you don't even have
         the slightest idea about what one must put up with in a
         job...'

(7.37) a. <u>Prácticamente</u> te veía en todos los rostros de mujer y todas
         las voces me parecían la tuya (175).
         'I would see you practically in every woman's face, and
         every voice seemed to be yours.'

      b. Recordá que Quesada era <u>prácticamente</u> un hombre feliz (123).
         'Remember that Quesada was practically a happy man.'

(7.38) a. Siempre he apreciado mucho a Quesada y <u>precisamente</u> creí
         que sería valioso cerca de la dirección...(120)
         'I've always been very fond of Quesada and I thought that
         he would be useful close to the director...'

      b. Ahora vas a salir con obsesiones. <u>Precisamente</u> eso te pasa
         en el trabajo. ¡Pensás demasiado! (98).
         'Now you're going to start with your obsessions. It is pre-
         cisely that what happens to you at work. You think too much!'

(7.39) a. <u>Simplemente</u> quiero expresarle mi solidaridad en esta amarga
         hora...(126)
         'I simply want to express my solidarity with you in this
         bitter hour...'

      b. ...eso puede ser <u>simplemente</u> un oficio (134).
         '...that may be just a craft.'

(7.40) a. No, <u>solamente</u> le decía lo que planeo hacer (33).
         'No, I was just telling you what I'm planning to do.'

      b. Pensaba <u>solamente</u> en cómo ayudar y servir al prójimo (127).
         'I was just thinking of how to help and serve my fellow
         human beings.'

(7.41) a. ¡Qué alma tendría yo si <u>sólo</u> pensara en vender y comprar
         cosas...(96)
         'What kind of soul would I have if I only thought of selling
         and buying things...'

      b. ...en la mañana me dijiste que vendrías <u>sólo</u> a comer (97).
         '...this morning you told me that you would come only to
         eat.'

(7.42) a. Lo que pasa es que <u>ya</u> casi están enterrando a Quesada (132).
         'What happens is that they are already almost burying Que-
         sada.'

      b. ...tu ropa <u>ya</u> tiene brillo...(100)
         '...your clothes are beginning to shine...'

I will assume that these adjuncts are entered in the lexicon with a contextual feature specifying that they can be inserted in the environment of en element marked [+rheme]. Since these adjuncts normally precede the rheme, this contextual feature will require them to be so placed, i.e. the feature will be +[___ [+rheme]].

Some of the adjuncts in this class may also appear after the rheme, as shown by the sentences in (7.43),

(7.43) a. Hay gente que ni sufre, ni goza, que vive <u>nada más</u> (115).
'There are people who do not suffer or are happy, people who just live.'

b. ...es un hombre totalmente embargado entre una plata que entra y otra que sale, sin que alcance <u>casi</u> para lo más necesario (93).
'...one is a man who is totally trapped between some incoming and some outgoing money, almost not enough for one's essential needs.'

c. Me doy por vencido, no encuentro <u>todavía</u> la forma de hacerte comprender...(114)
'I give up, I still don't find the way to make you understand...'

and some may also occur in the middle of the rhematic string which they help identify, as in (7.44).

(7.44) a. Calculo que hemos <u>ya</u> ahorrado una cantidad muy representativa (34).
'I estimate that we have already saved a very representative amount.'

b. Cuando aceptamos un hueso, vendemos <u>prácticamente</u> el alma al diablo (165).
'When we accept a bone, we practically sell our souls to the devil.'

This indicates the need for additional rules to move rhematizers from their basic pre-rhematic position. These rules will be discussed in chapter twelve.

7.5 Conclusions

Let us now summarize our analysis of adjuncts by means of the following diagram:

(7.45)

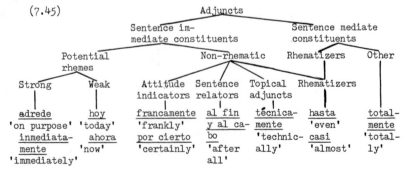

Potential rhemes, as the name indicates, may be treated as new information; in the terms of our grammar, they may be assigned the feature
[+rheme]. 'Strong' potential rhemes, like adrede 'on purpose', are at the
top of the RSH, whereas 'weak' potential rhemes like hoy 'today' are at
the bottom.

Among the non-rhematic adjuncts, we have referred briefly to attitude
indicators, sentence relators and topical adjuncts, and in more detail
to rhematizers. Since the latter occur normally directly followed by the
rheme, we have suggested that they be entered in the lexicon with the following contextual feature: +[___ [+rheme]]. Their occurrence in other
positions will be accounted for by rules discussed in chapter twelve.

Finally, the adjuncts on the far right column in (7.45) fall outside
the scope of this study.

FOOTNOTES TO CHAPTER SEVEN

[1]All page numbers in this chapter refer to Naranjo 1974.

Chapter Eight

NORMAL ORDER

In this chapter, we will examine the rules which assign a linear order to sentence constituents on the basis of their rhematic status. We will
limit ourselves here to normal word order, emphatic order being the subject of a later chapter. Also excluded from this chapter, but dealt with
later, is the order determined by factors other than rhematic structure.

8.1 Linear order rules

Let us begin by considering semantic structure (8.1).

(8.1) $\{$[+rheme], empezó,   la resistencia$\}$
                Predicate   Patient
                'started'   'the resistance'

If the feature [+rheme] is assigned to the patient only, the normal
order of the resulting sentence will be as in (8.2).

(8.2) Empezó la resistencia.

If, on the other hand, the feature [+rheme] is assigned only to the
predicate, the normal order is as in (8.3).

(8.3) La resistencia empezó.

The grammar must, then, include a rule that places the rheme to the
right of the theme, as follows:

(8.4) LINEAR ORDER I (OBLIGATORY)

$$\left\{ \begin{array}{cc} X & Y \\ [-rheme] & [+rheme] \\ 1 & 2 \end{array} \right\} \rightarrow 1 + 2$$

Let us recall, however, that the rule of rheme assignment may attach
the feature [+rheme] to more than one constituent. What is the normal order then, in our example, if both constituents are rhematic? In other
words, how are the constituents ordered for the sentence to be interpreted
as an appropriate answer to question (8.5)?

(8.5) ¿Qué pasó?
     'What happened?'

The order in this case is, of course, as in (8.2).
Let us recall that according to rule (6.16) the patient la resistencia ranks lower in the RSH than the presentational predicate empezó. This
indicates that, in order to predict the right linear order for the answer
to question (8.5) we need a rule that places a higher ranking rheme to the
right of a lower ranking rheme, as follows:

(8.6) LINEAR ORDER II (OBLIGATORY) - Tentative

$$\left\{ \begin{array}{cc} X & Y \\ [+rheme] & [+rheme] \\ 1 & 2 \end{array} \right\} \rightarrow 1 + 2$$

Condition: 2 ranks higher than 1 in the RSH

The combined effect of rules (8.4) and (8.6) is to order rhemes to
the right of themes, and higher ranking rhemes to the right of lower ranking rhemes. So far, our grammar does not assign any linear order to a
sequence of non-rhematic elements. We will deal with this problem later
in this chapter.

8.1.1 Application of rules to two-argument sentences

Let us see now how our rules apply to more complex structures, beginning with two-argument sentences like the following:

(8.7) $\begin{Bmatrix} \text{está procurando,} & \text{ella,} & \text{enseñarte} \\ \text{Predicate} & \text{Agent} & \text{Patient} \\ \text{'is trying'} & \text{'she'} & \text{'to teach you'} \end{Bmatrix}$

Let us assume that the feature [+rheme] is assigned to the predicate
and the patient, but not to the agent. Rule (8.4) will place the two rhemes
to the right of the non-rhematic agent, and rule (8.6) will place the
patient to the right of the predicate, according to the rhematic hierarchy
established by rule (6.16). The resulting string is, then, the following:

(8.8) Ella está procurando enseñarte.
      'She is trying to teach you.'

Once the main sentential stress has been assigned to the last constituent, by a rule to be discussed later, this sentence is in effect an appropriate answer to question (8.9),

(8.9) ¿Qué hace ella?
      'What is she doing?'

which establishes the agent ella 'she' as a theme.
      Let us assume now that the rule of rheme assignment converts semantic
structure (8.7) into rhematic structure (8.10).

(8.10) $\begin{Bmatrix} \text{está procurando,} & \text{ella,} & \text{enseñarte} \\ \text{Predicate} & \text{Agent} & \text{Patient} \\ [\text{-rheme}] & [\text{+rheme}] & [\text{-rheme}] \end{Bmatrix}$

In this case, rule (8.4) will place the agent to the right of the
other two constituents, and rule (8.6) will not apply, since there is only
one rhematic constituent. In the absence of a rule that assigns a linear
order to a sequence of thematic elements, this structure adopts either
form (8.11) or form (8.12), after the assignment of sentential stress:

(8.11) Está procurando enseñarte ELLA.
       'SHE is trying to teach you.'

(8.12) Enseñarte está procurando ELLA.
       ·'SHE is trying to teach you.'

This does not seem adequate, however, since (8.11) is clearly a more
adequate answer to question (8.13) than (8.12).[1]

(8.13) ¿Quién está procurando enseñarme?
       'Who is trying to teach me?'

We must add a rule, then, to establish a linear order between thematic elements. Let us consider another example that will be helpful in determining the form of such a rule. Let us assume that the rule of rheme assignment has converted semantic structure (8.7) into rhematic structure
(8.14).

(8.14) $\left\{\begin{array}{lll} \text{está procurando,} & \text{ella,} & \text{enseñarte} \\ \text{Predicate} & \text{Agent} & \text{Patient} \\ [\text{-rheme}] & [\text{-rheme}] & [\text{+rheme}] \end{array}\right\}$

In the absence of a rule to order themes with respect to one another, this structure will adopt either order (8.15) or order (8.16).

(8.15) Ella está procurando ENSEÑARTE.
'She is trying to TEACH you.'

(8.16) Está procurando ella ENSEÑARTE.
'She is trying to TEACH you.'

But again only the first of these two sentences is an appropriate answer to the pertinent question, namely (8.17).

(8.17) ¿Qué está procurando ella?
'What is trying to do?'

On the basis of these two examples, it is possible to determine the form of the rule that assigns an order to sequences of thematic elements. Notice that the right sequences (8.11) and (8.15) show the order predicate + patient and agent + predicate respectively, while the inadequate sequences (8.12) and (8.16) show the opposite order. Recalling the rhematic hierarchy established in chapters five and six, we see that in the correct cases the theme on the right ranks higher than the theme on the left. In other words, themes are ordered with respect to each other by the same principle of rhematic hierarchy than rhemes. The rule, then, looks like this:

(8.18) LINEAR ORDER III (OBLIGATORY) - Tentative

$$\left\{\begin{array}{cc} X & Y \\ [\text{-rheme}] & [\text{-rheme}] \\ 1 & 2 \end{array}\right\} \rightarrow 1 + 2$$

Condition: 2 ranks higher than 1 in the RSH

Since this rule differs from (8.6) only in the specification [-rheme], it is possible to combine them into one rule stating that in a sequence of themes or rhemes, the higher ranking element follows the lower ranking one. With the usual conventions of transformational grammar for such cases, the resulting rule looks like this:

(8.19) LINEAR ORDER II (OBLIGATORY) - Revised

$$\left\{\begin{array}{cc} X & Y \\ [\alpha\text{rheme}] & [\alpha\text{rheme}] \\ 1 & 2 \end{array}\right\} \rightarrow 1 + 2$$

Condition: 2 ranks higher than 1 in the RSH

Another rhematic structure derived from (8.7) is (8.20),

(8.20) $\left\{\begin{array}{lll} \text{está procurando,} & \text{ella,} & \text{enseñarte} \\ \text{Predicate} & \text{Agent} & \text{Patient} \\ [\text{-rheme}] & [\text{+rheme}] & [\text{+rheme}] \end{array}\right\}$

which generates the appropriate answer to question (8.21).

(8.21) ¿Quién está procurando qué?
'Who is trying to do what?'

The application of our linear rules, however, produces a sentence
which does not constitute an adequate answer to that question, namely
(8.22).

(8.22) Está procurando ella ENSEÑARTE.
       'She is trying to TEACH you.'

The correct surface structure corresponding to (8.20) is (8.23).

(8.23) ELLA está procurando ENSEÑARTE.
       'SHE is trying to TEACH you.'

This suggests the need for another rule that splits the rhematic
chain when the predicate is thematic, as follows:

(8.24) RHEME SPLITTING (OBLIGATORY)

$$
\begin{array}{ccc}
\text{Predicate} + & X & + \quad Y \\
[-\text{rheme}] & [+\text{rheme}] & [+\text{rheme}] \\[4pt]
1 & 2 & 3 \quad \rightarrow \\
2 + 1 & \emptyset & 3
\end{array}
$$

This rule, plus an appropriately stated rule of sentential stress
assignment, will generate sentence (8.23) as the surface structure corresponding to (8.20).
Another structure derived from (8.7) is (8.25),

(8.25) $\left\{ \begin{array}{lll} \text{está procurando,} & \text{ella,} & \text{enseñarte} \\ \text{Predicate} & \text{Agent} & \text{Patient} \\ [+\text{rheme}] & [+\text{rheme}] & [-\text{rheme}] \end{array} \right\}$

which the rules of linear order, plus the rule of sentential stress assignment, convert into sequence (8.26).

(8.26) Enseñarte ella está PROCURANDO.
       'She is TRYING to teach you.'

However, this sentence is not a particularly felicitous answer to
the question it is supposed to answer, namely (8.27).

(8.27) ¿Qué hay con eso de 'enseñarme'?
       'What about this business of "teaching me"?'

There seem to be special factors determining the low acceptability
of sentences like this, which will be explored in chapter ten. Let us
just note for now that if the topical character of the predicate is marked
more clearly, as in (8.28), the sentence improves:

(8.28) En cuanto a enseñarte, ella está PROCURANDO hacerlo.
       'As for teaching you, she is TRYING to do it.'

Finally, semantic structure (8.7) generates rhematic structure (8.29).

(8.29) $\left\{ \begin{array}{lll} \text{está procurando,} & \text{ella,} & \text{enseñarte} \\ \text{Predicate} & \text{Agent} & \text{Patient} \\ [+\text{rheme}] & [+\text{rheme}] & [+\text{rheme}] \end{array} \right\}$

In this case, the rule which places higher ranking rhemes to the right
of lower ranking rhemes, plus the rule of sentential stress assignment,
produce the following surface structure:

(8.30) Ella está procurando ENSEÑARTE.
       'She is trying to TEACH you.'

which is, in fact, the appropriate answer to question (8.31).

(8.31) ¿Qué pasa?
     'What's up?'

Summing up, semantic structure (8.7) is related to the following rhematic structures, which the linear order rules convert into the sequences indicated:

(8.32)

Rhematic structures			Rules applied	Linear order
a. Predicate, [-rheme]	Agent, [+rheme]	Patient [+rheme]	(8.4), (8.19) (8.24)	Ag + Pred + Pat
b. Predicate, [-rheme]	Agent, [-rheme]	Patient [+rheme]	(8.4), (8.19)	Ag + Pred + Pat
c. Predicate, [-rheme]	Agent, [+rheme]	Patient [-rheme]	(8.4), (8.19)	Pred + Pat + Ag
d. Predicate, [+rheme]	Agent, [-rheme]	Patient [+rheme]	(8.4), (8.19)	Ag + Pred + Pat
e. Predicate, [+rheme]	Agent, [+rheme]	Patient [-rheme]	(8.4), (8.19)	Pat + Ag + Pred
f. Predicate, [+rheme]	Agent, [+rheme]	Patient [+rheme]	(8.19)	Ag + Pred + Pat

The sentential stress assignment rule, which will be discussed later, assigns the main stress to the last element of all these sentences. In the case of a, this rule must also assign a sentential stress to the agent. This means that cases b, d, and f are all represented by the following surface structure:

(8.33) Ella está procurando ENSEÑARTE.
     'She is trying to TEACH you.'

which adequately reflects the fact that this surface structure may answer any of the following questions:

(8.34) a. ¿Qué está procurando (hacer) ella? (case b)
       'What is she trying to do?'

     b. ¿Qué hace ella? (case d)
       'What is she doing?'

     c. ¿Qué hay? (case f)
       'What's up?'

On the other hand, surface structure (8.35) corresponds only to rhematic structure (8.32c),

(8.35) Está procurando enseñarte ELLA.
     'SHE is trying to teach you.'

which adequately reflects the fact that this sentence may only answer a question like (8.36).[2]

(8.36) ¿Quién está procurando enseñarme?
     'Who is trying to teach me?'

Similarly, surface structure (8.37) corresponds only to rhematic structure (8.32e),

(8.37) Enseñarte ella está PROCURANDO.
      'She is TRYING to teach you.'

which adequately reflects the fact that it only answers (although not too
felicitously, for reasons to be discussed in chapter ten) a question like
(8.38).

(8.38) ¿Qué hay con eso de "enseñarme"?
      'What about this business of "teaching me"?'

8.1.2 Application of rules to three-argument sentences

Let us now consider a semantic structure with three arguments, like
the following:

(8.39) $\left\{\begin{array}{llll} \text{sacó,} & \text{don Fermín, sus espuelas, de la sala} \\ \text{Predicate Agent} & \text{Patient} & \text{Source} \\ \text{'took'} & \text{'don Fermín' 'his spurs'} & \text{'from the room'} \end{array}\right\}$

from which fifteen different rhematic structures may be derived.

Let us begin with the rhematic structures which do not violate the
rheme selection hierarchy:

(8.40) a. Predicate, Agent,   Patient, Source
         [+rheme]   [-rheme] [+rheme] [+rheme]

       b. Predicate, Agent,   Patient, Source
         [-rheme]   [-rheme] [+rheme] [+rheme]

       c. Predicate, Agent,   Patient, Source
         [-rheme]   [-rheme] [-rheme] [+rheme]

       d. Predicate, Agent,   Patient, Source
         [+rheme]   [+rheme] [+rheme] [+rheme]

All of these structures, through the application of rules (8.4) and
(8.19) plus the rule of sentential stress assignment, are converted into
the following surface structure:

(8.41) Don Fermín (ag) sacó (pred) sus espuelas (pat) de la SALA (so).
      'Don Fermín took his spurs from the ROOM.'

Thus, our rules predict accurately that (8.41) may answer any of the
questions in (8.42).

(8.42) a. ¿Qué hizo don Fermín?
         'What did don Fermín do?'

       b. ¿Qué sacó don Fermín y de dónde?
         'What did don Fermín take and from where?'

       c. ¿De dónde sacó don Fermín sus espuelas?
         'Where did don Fermín take his spurs from?'

       d. ¿Qué pasó?
         'What happened?'

As for the rest of the structures derived from (8.39), we will consider first the atypical rhematic structures which have only one rheme:

(8.43) a. Predicate, Agent,   Patient, Source
         [-rheme]   [-rheme] [+rheme] [-rheme]

     b. Predicate, Agent,   Patient, Source
       [-rheme] [+rheme] [-rheme] [-rheme]

     c. Predicate, Agent,   Patient, Source
       [+rheme] [-rheme] [-rheme] [-rheme]

The linear order rules convert these structures into the following sequences respectively:

(8.44) a. Don Fermín (ag) sacó (pred) de la sala (so) sus ESPUELAS (pat).
      'Don Fermín took his SPURS from the room.'

     b. Sacó (pred) sus espuelas (pat) de la sala (so) don FERMÍN (ag).
      'Don FERMIN took his spurs from the room.'

     c. Don Fermín (ag) sus espuelas (pat) de la sala (so) SACÓ (pred).
      'Don Fermín TOOK his spurs from the room.'

However, none of these sentences is a completely adequate response to the relevant question, namely (8.45a), (8.45b), and (8.45c) respectively.

(8.45) a. ¿Qué sacó don Fermín de la sala?
      'What did don Fermín take from the room?'

     b. ¿Quién sacó sus espuelas de la sala?
      'Who took his spurs from the room?'

     c. ¿Qué hizo don Fermín en relación con sus espuelas y la sala?
      'What did don Fermín do with regard to his spurs and the room?'

More adequate than the sentences in (8.44) are the following:

(8.46) a. Don Fermín sacó sus ESPUELAS de la sala.
      'Don Fermín took his SPURS from the room.'

     b. Don FERMIN sacó sus espuelas de la sala.
      'Don FERMIN took his spurs from the room.'

     c. Don Fermín SACÓ sus espuelas de la sala.
      'Don Fermín TOOK his spurs from the room.'

In the less acceptable sentences of (8.44) all the thematic elements precede the rheme, whereas in (8.46) the only themes which precede the rheme are those that rank lower than it in the RSH. The principle by which the grammar signals the greater acceptability of (8.46) over (8.44) will be discussed in chapter ten.

Let us consider now the atypical rhematic structures derived from (8.39) by assigning rhematic status to two constituents:

(8.47) a. Predicate, Agent,   Patient, Source
       [+rheme] [+rheme] [-rheme] [-rheme]

     b. Predicate, Agent,   Patient, Source
       [+rheme] [-rheme] [+rheme] [-rheme]

     c. Predicate, Agent,   Patient, Source
       [+rheme] [-rheme] [-rheme] [+rheme]

d. Predicate, Agent,   Patient, Source
   [-rheme]   [+rheme] [+rheme] [-rheme]

e. Predicate, Agent,   Patient, Source
   [-rheme]   [+rheme] [-rheme] [+rheme]

The linear order rules convert these structures into the following sequences:

(8.48) a. Sus espuelas (pat) de la sala (so) don Fermín (ag) SACÓ (pred).
'It was don FERMIN who TOOK his spurs from the room.'

b. Don Fermín (ag) de la sala (so) sacó (pred) sus ESPUELAS (pat).
'It was his SPURS that don Fermín TOOK from the room.'

c. Don Fermín (ag) sus espuelas (pat) sacó (pred) de la SALA (so).
'His spurs don Fermín took from the ROOM.'

d. Sacó (pred) de la sala (so) don Fermín (ag) sus ESPUELAS (pat).
'Don FERMIN took his SPURS from the room.'

e. Sacó (pred) sus espuelas (pat) don Fermín (ag) de la SALA (so).
'Don FERMIN took his spurs from the ROOM.'

But these sentences are even less acceptable than those in (8.44). More appropriate representations of the relevant rhematic structures in (8.47) are the following sequences:

(8.49) a. Don Fermín SACÓ sus espuelas de la sala.

b. Don Fermín sacó sus ESPUELAS de la sala.

c. Don Fermín SACÓ sus espuelas de la SALA.

d. Don FERMÍN sacó sus ESPUELAS de la sala.

e. Don FERMÍN sacó sus espuelas de la SALA.

which differ from those in (8.48) in the same way in which the sentences in (8.46) differ from those in (8.44), that is, they do not include any thematic element preceding a lower ranking rheme.

On the basis of the structures examined so far, it could be objected that the linear order always seems to follow the rhematic hierarchy regardless of which elements are themes and which rhemes. In other words, in our example the preferred order is always agent + predicate + patient + source regardless of the rhematic structure of the sentence, and it seems uneconomical to assign a linear order on the basis of rhematic structure only to change it later to the order indicated. Our analysis, however, is justified for the following reasons:

a) In the case of two-constituent sentences, as we have seen, the order does not always follow the rhematic hierarchy, as sentences like the following show: La resistencia EMPEZÓ. 'The resistance STARTED.', No salió el SOL. 'The SUN didn't come out.'

b) There are other variants for the sentences in (8.49) where the linear order does not follow the rhematic hierarchy, and which can be obtained by the optional application of the THEME POSTPOSING rule (to be discussed in chapter ten) to elements which rank lower than the rheme, for

instance, the following, which are equivalent to (8.49b) and (8.49e) respectively:

    (8.50) a. Sacó sus ESPUELAS don Fermín de la sala.

          b. Don FERMÍN sacó de la SALA sus espuelas.

    c) When the pre-rhematic theme is topicalized, the resulting order,
which may not follow the rhematic hierarchy, is impeccable. That is the
case, for instance, with the following variant of (8.48a) where the patient sus espuelas has been topicalized and the source de la sala postposed:
Sus espuelas don Fermín las SACÓ de la sala.

    For these reasons, we believe that the order assigned by rules (8.4)
and (8.19) is correct.

    Let us now continue to examine the rhematic structures derived from
(8.39). These are the atypical structures with three rhematic elements:

    (8.51) a. Predicate, Agent,   Patient, Source
           [+rheme] [+rheme] [+rheme] [-rheme]

          b. Predicate, Agent,   Patient, Source
           [-rheme] [+rheme] [+rheme] [+rheme]

          c. Predicate, Agent,   Patient, Source
           [+rheme] [+rheme] [-rheme] [+rheme]

    The linear order rules, plus the rule of sentential stress assignment,
convert these structures into the following strings respectively:

    (8.52) a. De la sala (so) don Fermín (ag) sacó (pred) sus ESPUELAS
          (pat).
          'Don Fermín took his SPURS from the room.'

          b. Sacó (pred) don Fermín (ag) sus espuelas (pat) de la SALA
          (pat).
          'Don FERMÍN took his spurs from the ROOM.'

          c. Sus espuelas (pat) don Fermín (ag) sacó (pred) de la SALA
          (so).
          'His spurs don Fermín took from the ROOM.'

    Sentence (8.52a) is grammatical, but it is not the most appropriate
surface structure for (8.51a). Further discussion of this type of sentence
will be found in chapter ten.

    Sentence (8.52b) meets the structural description of rule (8.24),
which converts it into the correct surface structure Don FERMÍN sacó sus
espuelas de la SALA.

    Finally, sentence (8.52c), like (8.52a), is also of low acceptability
for the reasons which we have hinted at before and which will be dealt
with more fully in chapter ten.

    This concludes our analysis of the different rhematic structures
derived from semantic structure (8.39).

    In contrast with what happens in simpler structures, we have seen
that the order predicted by our rules in this case may result in sentences
with a low degree of acceptability.

    This fact should not be surprising, since the contexts which are ne-
cessary for most of the atypical structures with three or more constituents are far more contrived than those of sentences with a typical rheme
selection. Thus, while the appropriate context for a typical sentence like
(8.53) may be expressed by a simple question like (8.54),

(8.53) Don Fermín sacó   sus espuelas de la sala.
     Agent   Predicate Patient   Source
     [-rheme] [+rheme] [+rheme]   [+rheme]
     'Don Fermín took his spurs from the room.'

(8.54) ¿Qué hizo don Fermín?
     'What did don Fermín do?'

there is no question that expresses the context required by an atypical structure like (8.55) naturally.

(8.55) Don Fermín sacó   sus espuelas de la sala.
     Agent   Predicate Patient   Source
     [+rheme] [+rheme] [-rheme]   [-rheme]

Since an examination of structures with more than three arguments would not shed any new light on the operation of the rules of linear order proposed here, we refrain from engaging in it.

As for adjuncts, those which are potential rhemes behave, in general, like arguments for the purposes of linear order. Other adjuncts have greater freedom of occurrence, and will be dealt with in chapter twelve.

8.2 Conclusions

Two basic rules have been proposed to generate sentences with normal word order. The first one orders rhemes to the right of themes, and the second one orders higher ranking elements to the right of lower ranking elements.

In addition, a special rule of RHEME SPLITTING has been proposed, that places a non-rhematic predicate after the first element in a rhematic string.

These rules account adequately for a variety of cases. However, structures with three or more constituents and an atypical rheme selection show the need for a principle assigning degrees of acceptability. The discussion of this principle is presented in chapter ten.

FOOTNOTES TO CHAPTER EIGHT

[1] The emphatic version of sentence (8.11) is still more acceptable: ELLA está procurando enseñarte. Sentence (8.12) shows topicalization of the predicate, and its most appropriate use would be in a contrastive series like the following: Enseñarte está procurando ELLA; convencerte (está procurando) EL, etc. 'As for teaching you, SHE is trying to do it; as for convincing you, HE is, etc.'

[2] See footnote 1.

Chapter Nine

TOPICALIZATION

Topicalization consists of selecting a sentence constituent as 'topic' of the predication expressed by the sentence. This selection is formally marked either by moving the topicalized element to the initial position or, if it belongs in that position anyway, by separating it from the rest of the sentence by a pause and/or by preposing to it 'topicalizing' expressions like en cuanto a 'as for', hablando de 'speaking of', etc. In some cases, the topicalized element leaves a pronominal copy in its original position. Let us look at some examples, where the topic and the pronominal copy, if any, are underlined:

(9.1) a. Este gobierno estúpido, ¿qué es lo que pretende?
'This stupid government, what is it trying to do?'

b. En cuanto a la mujer, no hay duda que se la posterga.
'As for women, there is no doubt they are discriminated against.'

c. ¡Cómo ha llovido en estos últimos días! Y yo que perdí el paraguas en una tienda (Naranjo 16).
'The way it's rained these last days! And me, I lost my umbrella at a store.'

d. ...a un hermano por lo menos hay que escribirle una cuartilla (Naranjo 29).
'...a brother, you must at least write one page to.'

e. Y vos y yo y todos seguiremos el mismo camino (Naranjo 60).
'And you and I and everyone will follow the same path.'

f. Aquélla, la del viejito, esa sí que está aplastada (Naranjo 92).
'That one, the old man's, that one is really crushed.'

Those topics which are overtly marked by topicalizing expressions like en cuanto a 'as for', hablando de 'speaking of', etc. appear only in pre-rhematic position, as shown by the ungrammaticality of (9.2).

(9.2) *No hay duda que se la posterga, en cuanto a la mujer.
'There is no doubt they are discriminated against, as for women.'

On the other hand, a topic which is not preceded by a topicalizer may occur in post-rhematic position, as shown by (9.3).

(9.3) No hay duda que se la POSTERGA a la mujer.[1]
'There is no doubt they are DISCRIMINATED against, women (are).'

Topicalization is not limited to arguments, as shown by the following sentence with a topicalized predicate:

(9.4) En cuanto a vender, vendió hasta su CASA la pobre.
'As for selling, she even sold her HOUSE, the poor woman.'

Both topicalization and the emphatic location of a rheme are devices for giving prominence to a constituent. They are, however, quite distinct, as shown by the following examples, the first with topicalization, and the second with a rheme in emphatic position:

(9.5) a. Eso me lo dijiste AYER.
         'That, you said it to me YESTERDAY.'

      b. ESO me dijiste ayer.
         'You told me THAT yesterday.'

9.1 Topic selection

Let us consider first the problem of topic selection. As we have seen, any element may function as a topic. The only restriction is that it be non-rhematic.

If we assume that semantic structure includes a feature [+topic], the rule that selects a topic may be formulated simply thus:

(9.6) TOPIC ASSIGNMENT (OPTIONAL)

$$\left\{ \begin{array}{cc} [\text{+topic}], & X \\ & [\text{-rheme}] \\ 1 & 2 \end{array} \right\} \rightarrow$$

$$\emptyset \qquad \begin{bmatrix} 2 \\ 1 \end{bmatrix}$$

This rule says that the feature [+topic] may be optionally assigned to any element having the feature [-rheme]. The rule may apply to one or more elements. The following sentence, for instance, has been assigned two topics:

(9.7) En cuanto al dictador y al pueblo, éste lo repudia a aquél.
      'As for the dictator and the people, the latter repudiates the former.'

In the case of a complex sentence, the topicalized element may be either an immediate constituent of the matrix sentence or a constituent of the embedded clause. In (9.8), the topic is an immediate constituent of the matrix sentence,

(9.8) En cuanto a María, Pedro le dijo que se casaría con ella.
      'As for Mary, Peter told her that he would marry her.'

whereas in (9.9), the topic is a constituent of the embedded clause:

(9.9) En cuanto al dictador, dicen que el pueblo lo repudia.
      'As for the dictator, they say the people repudiate him.'

9.2 Topic placement

In relation to the question of linear order, we have observed that topics may occur initially or finally, but the latter position is not allowed if they are preceded by topicalizers. This seems to indicate that the basic position for topics, as for other thematic elements, is sentence-initial, and that the final position is special, 'marked'. We must formulate a rule, then, to place topics in initial position. The formulation of the conditions for postposing topics must be delayed until we can deal with the problem of emphatic order in all its aspects.

Before formulating the rule of topic placement, we must raise the question concerning the relationship between the topic and the rest of the sentence. Is the topic an ordinary constituent or is there something

special about it? The fact that topics are normally separated from the
rest of the sentence by a pause would seem to indicate that they have a
special status. More specifically, it would seem that the grammar should
insert a special kind of boundary between the topic and the rest of the
sentence for the phonological component to assign the pause and the appropriate intonation.

There is a convention in transformational grammar that allows us to
give the boundary between the topic and the rest of the sentence a special
status, namely the operation known as 'Chomsky-adjunction', which adjoins
an element X to an element Y generating another node Y which dominates
X + Y. Thus, for instance, given a structure like (9.10),

(9.10)

$$\begin{array}{c} A \\ \diagup\diagdown \\ x \quad w \end{array}$$

Chomsky-adjunction of a node y produces a structure like this:

(9.11)

$$\begin{array}{c} A \\ \diagup\diagdown \\ y \quad A \\ \quad \diagup\diagdown \\ \quad x \quad w \end{array}$$

This would seem to be the adequate mechanism for 'segregating' the
topic from the rest of the sentence. Consequently, the following formalization is proposed:

(9.12) TOPIC PLACEMENT (OBLIGATORY)

$$\begin{bmatrix} X & + & Y \\ & & [+\text{topic}] \end{bmatrix}_S$$
$$\quad 1 \qquad 2 \qquad \rightarrow$$

$$2 \,\#\, 1 \quad \begin{bmatrix} 2 \\ [+\text{pro}] \end{bmatrix}$$

This rule states that the topic is placed in sentence-initial position
and dominated by the node S and followed by a 'sister' constituent S which
includes the rest of the sentence. The rule also adds the feature $[+\text{pro}]$
to the topic in its original position, to account for the anaphoric element which we have noted in some sentences with topicalized constituents.
Those sentences which do not show an anaphoric element in surface structure are assumed to have undergone deletion rules.

Given a structure like (9.13), generated by the rules of rheme assignment, topic assignment, and linear order,

(9.13)

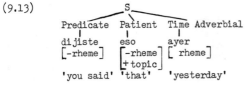

rule (9.12) changes it to (9.14).

(9.14)

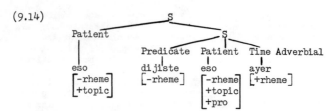

This structure, after stress assignment, pronoun insertion and 'cliticization' of the pronoun, becomes sentence (9.15).

(9.15) Eso lo dijiste AYER.
    'That, you said it YESTERDAY.'

In the case of a complex sentence, the topic may be either preposed to the main sentence, as in (9.16),

(9.16) En cuanto <u>al dictador</u>, dicen que el pueblo lo repudia.
    'As for the dictator, they say the people repudiate him.'

or to the embedded clause, as in (9.17).

(9.17) Dicen que <u>al dictador</u> el pueblo lo repudia.
    'They say that (as for) the dictator, the people repudiate him.'

The normal interpretation of the variable X in rule (9.12) allows for this double output.

9.3 Topicalization in non-declarative sentences

Although this study is limited to declarative sentences, we might note in passing that topicalization is also possible with interrogative, imperative and exclamatory sentences, as shown by the following examples:

(9.18) a. La CIA, ¿cuándo dejará de intervenir en los asuntos inter-
      nos de la América Latina?
      'The CIA, when will it stop meddling in the internal af-
      fairs of Latin America?'

     b. Ese libro, ¡quémalo al instante!
      'That book, burn it right away!'

     c. La mujer, ¡cómo se discrimina contra ella!
      'Women, the way they are discriminated against!'

9.4 Topicalization and pronominalization

Rule (9.12), with its insertion of the feature [+pro] under the original occurrence of the topicalized element, offers a natural explanation for a phenomenon often noted in Spanish grammars but never satisfactorily explained, namely the presence of a pronominal element in a sentence like (9.19) vis-à-vis its absence in a sentence like (9.20).

(9.19) Luces naturales no sé si las tengo (Hatcher 1956).
    'Natural lights, I don't know if I have them.'

(9.20) La reina de las Españas te mereces, hermoso (Hatcher 1956).
    'You deserve the Queen of the Spains, beautiful one.'

Hatcher notices that although most sentences with a pronominal copy like (9.19) have definite preposed objects, as in (9.21),

(9.21) a. A los necios hay que IGNORARLOS (Naranjo 44).
'Fools must be IGNORED.'

b. Perdón, señor, pero la señora que acaba de salir no podía dejarla con la palabra en la BOCA (Naranjo 45).
'Pardon me, sir, but the lady who just went out, I couldn't leave her without LISTENING to her.'

c. La labor de mi departamento la podía hacer hasta DORMIDO (Naranjo 53).
'The work of my department I could do even in my SLEEP.'

and most cases without a pronominal copy have indefinite preposed objects, as in (9.22),

(9.22) a. MUCHOS disgustos le proporcionaba aquella criatura (Hatcher 1956:34).
'That creature gave him MANY headaches.'

b. VERGUENZA les había de dar (Hatcher 1956:34).
'They should be ASHAMED of themselves.'

c. El perfecto hombre domesticado que ya hasta MANDADOS hace (Naranjo 165).
'The perfectly domesticated man who even runs ERRANDS.'

an explanation of the presence or absence of the pronoun on the basis of the definite or indefinite character of the preposed object is clearly not possible, in view of sentences like (9.19) and (9.20), where the correlation shown by the sentences in (9.21) and (9.22) does not exist.

Hatcher's picturesque description of examples like (9.20) and (9.22) as cases 'where the object flies up in the air like a balloon' and of examples like (9.19) and (9.21) as cases 'where [the object] is secured firmly to the ground' (Hatcher 1956:35), however, points in the right direction. In the less poetic terms of our analysis, the object in (9.19) and (9.21) has been topicalized, and its pronominal copy is an automatic consequence of that fact, as required by rule (9.12), whereas the initial element in (9.20) and (9.22) occupies that position by virtue of the rule of emphatic order, to be discussed in the next chapter, which postposes thematic elements. Once this rule and the one that assigns sentential stress have been presented, it will be clear that the difference between the two sentence types in question is an automatic consequence of their application plus that of the rules of topicalization.

There is one aspect of topicalization which still requires explanation. Notice that certain sentences with topics do not require a pronominal copy. Thus, for instance, sentence (9.19)

(9.19) Luces naturales no sé si las tengo.
'Natural lights, I don't know if I have them.'

may also occur as (9.23).

(9.23) Luces naturales no sé si tengo.
'Natural lights I don't know if I have.'

On the other hand, in sentences like those in (9.21), the pronominal copy is obligatory. In order to determine what distinguishes these sentences from (9.23), let us consider some other cases where the pronoun is optional:

> (9.24) a. Trigo no (lo) HAY en este país.
> 'Wheat we don't HAVE (it) in this country.'
>
> b. Dictadores (los) hay MUCHOS en nuestra pobre América.
> 'Dictators there are MANY in our poor America.'
>
> c. Burócratas no (los) NECESITO en este departamento.
> 'Beaurocrats I don't NEED (them) in this department.'

In all these cases, the preposed object has a generic meaning, and that seems to be the feature that allows the optional deletion of the pronominal copy. The same preposed objects, with a specific meaning, require the pronominal copy, as shown by the following examples:

> (9.25) a. El trigo no lo pude VENDER.
> b. *El trigo no pude VENDER.
> 'The wheat I couldn't SELL.'
>
> (9.26) a. Esos dictadores el pueblo los REPUDIA.
> b. *Esos dictadores el pueblo REPUDIA.
> 'Those dictators the people REPUDIATE.'
>
> (9.27) a. Los burócratas no los NECESITO en este departamento.
> b. *Los burócratas no NECESITO en este departamento.
> 'The beaurocrats I don't NEED in this department.'

The following optional rule accounts for this fact:

> (9.28) GENERIC PRONOUN DELETION (OPTIONAL)

$$\begin{bmatrix} +\text{topic} \\ +\text{pro} \\ +\text{generic} \end{bmatrix}$$

$$1 \rightarrow$$
$$\emptyset$$

It is a well known fact that subject pronouns may also be deleted in Spanish. This accounts for the possible absence of the anaphoric pronoun when the topicalized argument ends up being the subject of the sentence, as in (9.1a), repeated here:

> (9.1) a. Este gobierno estúpido, ¿qué es lo que pretende?
> 'This stupid government, what is it trying to do?'

9.5 Conclusions

This concludes our analysis of the process of topicalization. We have proposed a formal mechanism that accounts for the special character of the relationship between a topic and the rest of the sentence, and which allows the phonological component to insert the appropriate pause after the topic as well as to assign to it the right intonation. Our rule also accounts for the pronominal copy that appears in most sentences with topicalization.

The optional deletion of generic and subject pronouns is accounted for by special rules.

More will be said about the relationship between topicalization and emphatic order in the next chapter.

FOOTNOTES TO CHAPTER NINE

[1]This sentence, incidentally, illustrates the difference between topic
and theme. If the constituent a la mujer were only a postposed theme,
not a topic, the sentence would have the following form:
    (i) No hay duda que se POSTERGA a la mujer.
       'There is no doubt that women are DISCRIMINATED against.'
Section (9.4) presents this problem in more detail.

Chapter Ten

EMPHATIC ORDER

10.1 The rules

The linear order rules presented so far generate strings where the
highest ranking rheme occurs in final position. This is the normal order,
which, other factors being equal, has greater contextual freedom than
other orders. But we know that sentences may also appear in an 'emphatic'
order, where the highest ranking rheme does not occur in final position.
Thus, for instance, besides sentences (10.1) and (10.2), which are generated by our linear order rules,

    (10.1) Empezó la RESISTENCIA.
          'The RESISTANCE started.'

    (10.2) La resistencia EMPEZÓ.
          'The resistance STARTED.'

there occur sentences like (10.3) and (10.4).

    (10.3) EMPEZÓ la resistencia.
          'The resistance STARTED.'

    (10.4) La RESISTENCIA empezó.
          'The RESISTANCE started.'

We have seen in previous chapters that a sentence like (10.1) derives
from two different rhematic structures, one where only the patient la resistencia is rhematic, and one where both constituents are. On the other
hand, sentence (10.4), which is the mirror image of (10.1), derives only
from the former rhematic structure. This indicates that the rule which
relates these two sentences postposes only thematic elements. Such a formulation is compatible with the relationship between (10.2) and (10.3),
since in both of them the patient is interpreted as thematic.

As an approximation, let us formulate the pertinent rule like this:

    (10.5) THEME POSTPOSING (OPTIONAL)

$$\begin{array}{ccc} X & + & Y \\ [-\text{rheme}] & & [+\text{rheme}] \\ 1 & & 2 \qquad \rightarrow \\ \emptyset & & 2 + 1 \end{array}$$

Since the occurrence of emphatic sentences is limited to assertive
contexts, as shown in chapters one and three, the following condition
must be added to this rule:

    (10.6) THEME POSTPOSING is applicable only if the sentence is an
          assertion.

Let us consider a three-constituent structure like (10.7),

    (10.7) hice,   yo,   eso mismo
          Predicate Agent Patient
          [-rheme] [-rheme][+rheme]
          'did'   'I'   'the same thing'

which the rules of linear order convert into string (10.8).

    (10.8) yo   +   hice   +   eso mismo
           Agent   Predicate Patient
           [-rheme] [-rheme] [+rheme]

The application of rule (10.5) to this string produces the following
two sentences:

    (10.9) a. Eso MISMO hice yo.
          b. *Eso MISMO yo hice.
            'I did the SAME thing.'

of which only the first is grammatical.

    The same situation holds for more complex structures like the follow-
ing:

    (10.10) ⎧ sacó,   don Fermín,   sus espuelas, de la sala   ⎫
          ⎨ Predicate Agent   Patient   Source   ⎬
          ⎩ [-rheme] [-rheme]   [-rheme]   [+rheme]   ⎭
            'took'   'don Fermín' 'his spurs'   'from the room'

The linear order rules convert this structure into the following
string,

    (10.11) Don Fermín + sacó   + sus espuelas + de la sala
           Agent   Predicate Patient   Source
           [-rheme]   [-rheme] [-rheme]   [+rheme]

which rule (10.5) optionally transforms into one of the following strings,

    (10.12) a. De la SALA sacó don Fermín sus espuelas.

          b. De la SALA sacó sus espuelas don Fermín.

          c. *De la SALA sus espuelas don Fermín sacó.

          d. *De la SALA don Fermín sus espuelas sacó.

          e. *De la SALA don Fermín sacó sus espuelas.

          f. *De la SALA sus espuelas sacó don Fermín.

all of which, except the first two, are ungrammatical.

    Comparing examples (10.9) and (10.12), we see that, although the or-
der of the post-rhematic arguments is indifferent, the postposed predicate
must follow the rheme directly. To insure this result we might either
modify the rule of THEME POSTPOSING or add an ad-hoc rule to place the
predicate in the right position after it has been postposed. We opt for
the second alternative for reasons that will become clear in chapter
twelve. At this point, let us just say that there is an interesting
parallelism between the rule of THEME POSTPOSING and another reordering
rule which can only be captured if the former is left in its unmodified
version and the position of the post-rhematic predicate is determined by
an independent rule.

    Consequently, we add the following rule to our grammar:

    (10.13) POSTPOSED PREDICATE MOVEMENT (OBLIGATORY)

$$
\begin{array}{ccccc}
X & + & Y & + & Z \\
[+\text{rheme}] & & [-\text{rheme}] & & \text{Predicate} \\
& & & & [-\text{rheme}] \\
1 & & 2 & & 3 \rightarrow \\
1 + 3 & & 2 & & \emptyset
\end{array}
$$

This rule changes the ungrammatical sequences in (10.9) and (10.12) into the corresponding grammatical sequences. The linear order of the rest of the postposed thematic elements is indifferent, and rule (10.5) adequately accounts for this fact, since the variable X may stand for one or more constituents.

Besides the sentences given in (10.12), rhematic structure (10.10) may be transformed into the following sequences, given the optionality of rule (10.5):

(10.14) a. Don Fermín sacó de la SALA sus espuelas.

       b. *Don Fermín de la SALA sacó sus espuelas.

       c. Sacó sus espuelas de la SALA don Fermín.

       d. *Sus espuelas de la SALA sacó don Fermín.

       e. *Don Fermín sus espuelas de la SALA sacó.

These examples indicate that it is not possible to postpose the predicate without postposing also all the thematic arguments. It becomes necessary, then, to add a condition to rule (10.5) making obligatory the postposition of all the thematic arguments when the predicate is postposed.

Notice, however, that this condition does not affect a topicalized theme, as shown by the grammaticality of (10.15).

(10.15) Sus espuelas de la SALA las sacó don Fermín.
       'His spurs don Fermín took from the ROOM.'

The condition which accounts for these facts must, then, be formulated like this:

(10.16) If element X in rule (10.5) includes the predicate, it must also include all other elements with the features [-rheme, -topic].

Let us now consider rhematic structure (10.17),

(10.17)
$$\left\{ \begin{array}{llll} \text{sacó,} & \text{don Fermín,} & \text{sus espuelas,} & \text{de la sala} \\ \text{Predicate} & \text{Agent} & \text{Patient} & \text{Source} \\ [\text{-rheme}] & [\text{+rheme}] & [\text{-rheme}] & [\text{-rheme}] \\ \text{'took'} & \text{'don Fermín'} & \text{'his spurs'} & \text{'from the room'} \end{array} \right\}$$

which the linear order rules convert into sequence (10.18).

(10.18) Sacó sus espuelas de la sala don FERMÍN.
       'Don FERMÍN took his spurs from the room.'

As we saw in chapter eight, this sentence is not the appropriate answer to question (10.19),

(10.19) ¿Quién sacó sus espuelas de la sala?
       'Who took his spurs from the room?'

but emphatic version (10.20) is.

(10.20) Don FERMÍN sacó sus espuelas de la sala.
       'Don FERMÍN took his spurs from the room.'

This would seem to suggest that THEME POSTPOSING is obligatory for certain structures. Alternatively, we might say that the deviance of strings like (10.18) is a stylistic matter explainable in terms of a surface structure constraint.

In the next section, we will attempt to show that the second alternative is the correct one.

10.2 THEME POSTPOSING and the RSH

Let us consider structure (10.21), which is parallel to (10.17).

(10.21)
$$\left\{ \begin{array}{llll}
\text{cerró,} & \text{María,} & \text{la puerta,} & \text{con llave} \\
\text{Predicate} & \text{Agent} & \text{Patient} & \text{Instrument} \\
\text{[-rheme]} & \text{[+rheme]} & \text{[-rheme]} & \text{[-rheme]} \\
\text{'closed'} & \text{'Mary'} & \text{'the door'} & \text{'with a key'}
\end{array} \right\}$$

Just as in the case of (10.17), the string resulting from the application of the linear order rules, namely (10.22),

(10.22) ?Cerró la puerta con llave MARÍA.
         'MARY locked the door.'

is less acceptable than the version which has undergone postposition of all the thematic elements:

(10.23) MARÍA cerró la puerta con llave.
         'MARY locked the door.'

If we ask what sequences (10.18) and (10.22) have in common, we will see that the rheme is actually the lowest ranking element in the rheme-selection hierarchy (see chapter five). A reasonable solution would be to add a condition to rule (10.5) making its application obligatory to any theme ranking higher than the rheme. This condition, however, is too strong, since in a structure like (10.24),

(10.24)
$$\left\{ \begin{array}{llll}
\text{sacó,} & \text{don Fermín,} & \text{sus espuelas,} & \text{de la sala} \\
\text{Predicate} & \text{Agent} & \text{Patient} & \text{Source} \\
\text{[-rheme]} & \text{[-rheme]} & \text{[+rheme]} & \text{[-rheme]}
\end{array} \right\}$$

which has a theme, de la sala, that ranks higher than the rheme, this theme is not obligatorily postposed; that is, both of the following versions are grammatical, the second one being slightly more acceptable:

(10.25) a. Don Fermín sacó de la sala sus ESPUELAS.
         b. Don Fermín sacó sus ESPUELAS de la sala.
            'Don Fermín took his SPURS from the room.'

The same is true of our other example. Given a structure like (10.26),

(10.26)
$$\left\{ \begin{array}{llll}
\text{cerró,} & \text{María,} & \text{la puerta,} & \text{con llave} \\
\text{Predicate} & \text{Agent} & \text{Patient} & \text{Instrument} \\
\text{[-rheme]} & \text{[-rheme]} & \text{[+rheme]} & \text{[-rheme]}
\end{array} \right\}$$

both of the following versions are grammatical, although the second one is more acceptable:

(10.27) a. María cerró con llave la PUERTA.
         b. María cerró la PUERTA con llave.
            'Mary locked the DOOR with a key.'

The difference between sentences (10.25a) and (10.27a) on the one hand, and sentences (10.18) and (10.22) on the other, is that in the former there is only one thematic element which outranks the rheme whereas in the latter there are three. This makes the former more acceptable than the latter. The fully acceptable sentences (10.25b) and (10.27b) have no theme outranking the rheme in pre-rhematic position.

Let us consider now a structure with two thematic constituents which
outrank the rheme:

(10.28) $\begin{cases} \text{pronunció,} & \text{María,} & \text{un discurso} \\ \text{Predicate} & \text{Agent} & \text{Patient} \\ \text{[-rheme]} & \text{[+rheme]} & \text{[-rheme]} \\ \text{'pronounced'} & \text{'Mary'} & \text{'a speech'} \end{cases}$

Just as in cases (10.17) and (10.21), the postposition of both thematic elements would seem to be required:

(10.29) a. MARÍA pronunció un discurso.

       b. ?Pronunció un discurso MARÍA.

       c. ?Pronunció MARÍA un discurso.[1]
         'MARY gave a speech.'

If we were to deal with these cases by means of a modification of
the rule of THEME POSTPOSING making it obligatorily for certain structures, we would face the following problems:
     a) an arbitrary decision would have to be made regarding the exact
formulation of the proposed change: is THEME POSTPOSING obligatory in the
case of two or in the case of three or more pre-rhematic themes which outrank the rheme?;
     b) however the above question is resolved, the resulting condition
is fairly irregular: grammatical rules just do not operate on the basis
of statements like 'two or more X's';
     c) the gradual nature of the phenomenon in question would not be
captured.
     What we have is more characteristic of stylistic phenomena than of
grammatical rules. There is a scale of decreasing acceptability that goes
from fully acceptable sentences like (10.25b) and (10.29a) to less acceptable sentences like (10.25a) and (10.27a) to even less acceptable sentences like (10.29b) until we reach the least acceptable of all, namely
(10.18) and (10.22).
     The gradual nature of this phenomenon suggests that the adequate
formal device to deal with it is, not a grammatical rule, but a surface
structure constraint, such as those proposed by Ross (1967c) and Perlmutter (1971). Tentatively, we propose the following formulation:

(10.30) The acceptability of surface structures decreases
         as the number of pre-rhematic themes which outrank
         the rheme in the RSH increases.

This condition, which when appropriately refined will account for the
cases examined in this chapter, also explains the anomaly of the sequences
considered in chapter eight (examples (8.44) to (8.53)).
     We will examine these cases again, starting with those containing
only one rhematic element:

(8.44) a. $\begin{cases} \text{sacó,} & \text{don Fermín,} & \text{sus espuelas,} & \text{de la sala} \\ \text{Predicate} & \text{Agent} & \text{Patient} & \text{Source} \\ \text{[-rheme]} & \text{[-rheme]} & \text{[+rheme]} & \text{[-rheme]} \end{cases}$

       b. $\begin{cases} \text{sacó,} & \text{don Fermín,} & \text{sus espuelas,} & \text{de la sala} \\ \text{Predicate} & \text{Agent} & \text{Patient} & \text{Source} \\ \text{[-rheme]} & \text{[+rheme]} & \text{[-rheme]} & \text{[-rheme]} \end{cases}$

c. $\left\{\begin{array}{llll} \text{sacó,} & \text{don Fermín,} & \text{sus espuelas,} & \text{de la sala} \\ \text{Predicate} & \text{Agent} & \text{Patient} & \text{Source} \\ \text{[+rheme]} & \text{[-rheme]} & \text{[-rheme]} & \text{[-rheme]} \end{array}\right\}$

The first two of these cases are parallel to examples (10.17) and (10.24) and require no further comment. Structure (8.44c) is converted into sequence (10.31) by the linear order rules.

(10.31) Don Fermín sus espuelas de la sala SACÓ.
        'Don Fermín TOOK his spurs from the room.'

Surface structure constraint (10.30) predicts low acceptability for this sequence, since it contains two pre-rhematic themes, the patient sus espuelas and the source de la sala, which outrank the rheme sacó. This is an adequate prediction, as is the one that says that version (10.32), with no pre-rhematic theme outranking the rheme,

(10.32) Don Fermín SACÓ sus espuelas de la sala.
        'Don Fermín TOOK his spurs from the room.'

is perfectly acceptable.

Let us reconsider now the atypical cases including two rhematic elements:

(8.48) a. $\left\{\begin{array}{llll} \text{sacó,} & \text{don Fermín,} & \text{sus espuelas,} & \text{de la sala} \\ \text{Predicate} & \text{Agent} & \text{Patient} & \text{Source} \\ \text{[+rheme]} & \text{[+rheme]} & \text{[-rheme]} & \text{[-rheme]} \end{array}\right\}$

b. $\left\{\begin{array}{llll} \text{sacó,} & \text{don Fermín,} & \text{sus espuelas,} & \text{de la sala} \\ \text{Predicate} & \text{Agent} & \text{Patient} & \text{Source} \\ \text{[+rheme]} & \text{[-rheme]} & \text{[+rheme]} & \text{[-rheme]} \end{array}\right\}$

c. $\left\{\begin{array}{llll} \text{sacó,} & \text{don Fermín,} & \text{sus espuelas,} & \text{de la sala} \\ \text{Predicate} & \text{Agent} & \text{Patient} & \text{Source} \\ \text{[+rheme]} & \text{[-rheme]} & \text{[-rheme]} & \text{[+rheme]} \end{array}\right\}$

d. $\left\{\begin{array}{llll} \text{sacó,} & \text{don Fermín,} & \text{sus espuelas,} & \text{de la sala} \\ \text{Predicate} & \text{Agent} & \text{Patient} & \text{Source} \\ \text{[-rheme]} & \text{[+rheme]} & \text{[+rheme]} & \text{[-rheme]} \end{array}\right\}$

e. $\left\{\begin{array}{llll} \text{sacó,} & \text{don Fermín,} & \text{sus espuelas,} & \text{de la sala} \\ \text{Predicate} & \text{Agent} & \text{Patient} & \text{Source} \\ \text{[-rheme]} & \text{[+rheme]} & \text{[-rheme]} & \text{[+rheme]} \end{array}\right\}$

These structures are converted into the following respective sequences by the linear order rules:

(8.49) a. Sus espuelas (pat) de la sala (so) don Fermín (ag) SACÓ (pred).
          'It was don FERMÍN who TOOK his spurs from the room.'[2]

b. Don Fermín (ag) de la sala (so) sacó (pred) sus ESPUELAS (pat).
   'It was his SPURS that don Fermín TOOK from the room.'

c. Don Fermín (ag) sus espuelas (pat) sacó (pred) de la SALA (so).
   'His spurs don Fermín took from the ROOM.'

d. Sacó (pred) de la sala (so) don Fermín (ag) sus ESPUELAS (pat).
   'Don FERMÍN took his SPURS from the room.'

e. Sacó (pred) sus espuelas (pat) don Fermín (ag) de la SALA (so).
   'Don FERMÍN took his spurs from the ROOM.'

The low acceptability of (8.49a) is adequately predicted by surface structure constraint (10.30), since it contains two pre-rhematic themes, sus espuelas and de la sala, which outrank the rhemes don Fermín and sacó. The acceptability of this sentence, as predicted by constraint (10.30), increases as more thematic elements are postposed. Thus, version (10.33a) is more acceptable than either (10.33b) or (10.33c).

(10.33) a. Don Fermín SACÓ sus espuelas de la sala.

b. De la sala don Fermín SACÓ sus espuelas.

c. Sus espuelas don Fermín SACÓ de la sala.

Sentence (8.49b), on the other hand, is not as deviant as (8.49a), since it contains only one pre-rhematic theme which outranks the rhemes, namely the source de la sala. As predicted by condition (10.30), its acceptability increases even more when this theme is postposed:

(10.34) Don Fermín sacó sus ESPUELAS de la sala.

Similarly, (8.49c) is less deviant than (8.49a) because it only contains one pre-rhematic theme, the patient las espuelas, which outranks one of the rhematic elements, the predicate sacó, although it does not outrank the source de la sala.
(8.49d), on the other hand, is just as deviant as (8.49a), in accordance with principle (10.30): the theme sacó outranks the rheme don Fermín, and the theme de la sala outranks both rhemes, don Fermín and sus espuelas. Principle (10.30) predicts accurately the fact that the following versions of (8.49d) are more acceptable:

(10.35) a. Don FERMÍN sacó de la sala sus ESPUELAS.

b. Don FERMÍN sacó sus ESPUELAS de la sala.

Version (10.36) is disallowed by our grammar,

(10.36) *Sacó don Fermín sus ESPUELAS de la sala.

since the RHEME-SPLITTING rule (8.24) converts it obligatorily into (10.35b).
Also disallowed is version (10.37),

(10.37) *De la sala don Fermín sus ESPUELAS sacó.

since condition (10.16) requires that all non-topical thematic arguments be postposed if the predicate is.
Finally, principle (10.30) accurately predicts that sentence (9.49e) is deviant, since both the themes sacó and sus espuelas outrank the rheme don Fermín, although they do not outrank the rheme de la sala.
We have seen how principle (10.30) marks the sentences in (8.49) as less acceptable than the variants where one or more of the pre-rhematic themes are postposed. We have also noticed that, according to this principle, sentences (8.49b) and (8.49c) are less deviant than the rest, since they only contain one element which violates the rhematic hierarchy.
The question might be raised whether there are finer differences than these in the degree of acceptability of the sentences in (8.49). This is a difficult matter to decide, since it calls for extremely subtle distinctions. It is interesting, however, that a slight change

in the formulation of principle (10.30) allows us to establish finer distinctions in acceptability, which, at least in our judgment, correspond
to real intuitive differences.

Let us say that each case of a non-topical theme preceding a lower
ranking rheme constitutes one violation of the rhematic hierarchy, and
let us reformulate principle (10.30) like this:

(10.38) The acceptability of a sentence decreases in inverse
        proportion to the number of violations of the rhematic
        hierarchy.

In the light of this new principle, let us consider the sentences in
(8.49) once more:

(8.49) a. Sus espuelas de la sala don Fermín SACÓ.
          Patient   Source   Agent   Predicate
          [-rheme]   [-rheme]   [+rheme]   [+rheme]

       b. Don Fermín de la sala sacó   sus ESPUELAS.
          Agent   Source   Predicate Patient
          [-rheme]   [-rheme] [+rheme] [+rheme]

       c. Don Fermín sus espuelas sacó   de la SALA.
          Agent   Patient   Predicate Source
          [-rheme]   [-rheme]   [+rheme]   [+rheme]

       d. Sacó   de la sala don Fermín sus ESPUELAS.
          Predicate Source   Agent   Patient
          [-rheme] [-rheme]   [+rheme]   [+rheme]

       e. Sacó   sus espuelas don Fermín de la SALA.
          Predicate Patient   Agent   Source
          [-rheme] [-rheme]   [+rheme]   [+rheme]

Sentence (8.49a) shows the following violations of the rhematic
hierarchy:
1) The theme sus espuelas outranks the rheme don Fermín;
2) The theme sus espuelas outranks the rheme sacó;
3) The theme de la sala outranks the rheme don Fermín;
4) The theme de la sala outranks the rheme sacó.
Sentence (8.49b) presents two violations of the rhematic hierarchy:
1) The theme de la sala outranks the rheme sacó;
2) The theme de la sala outranks the rheme sus espuelas.
Sentence (8.49c) shows only one violation of the rhematic hierarchy:
1) The theme sus espuelas outranks the rheme sacó.
Sentence (8.49d) shows three violations:
1) The theme sacó outranks the rheme don Fermín;
2) The theme de la sala outranks the rheme don Fermín;
3) The theme de la sala outranks the rheme sus espuelas.
Finally, sentence (8.49e) contains two violations:
1) The theme sacó outranks the rheme don Fermín;
2) The theme sus espuelas outranks the rheme don Fermín.
According to this analysis, the sentences in question show the following scale of increasing acceptability:
a) (8.49a) - four violations;
b) (8.49d) - three violations;
c) (8.49b) and (8.49e) - two violations;
d) (8.49c) - one violation.

This agrees in general with our intuitive judgment of these sentences. A couple of cases requires further comment, however. Contrary
to the prediction made by principle (10.38), sentence (8.49e) seems to
us less acceptable than (8.49b), and sentence (8.49c) seems no more acceptable than (8.49b). Searching for a possible explanation of these
facts, we notice that the two rhemes in (8.49b), the predicate sacó
and the patient sus espuelas occupy contiguous ranks according to RSH
(7.31) and the special rule for the predicate (5.64), reproduced here
for convenience,

   (7.31) RHEME SELECTION HIERARCHY

         1. Instrument, manner adverbial, 'strong' time and place
            adverbial

         2. Target

         3. Complement, source, location, time, identifier, beneficiary

         4. Patient

         5. Agent, cause, possessor, experiencer

         6. 'Weak' time and place adverbial

   (5.64) The predicate always ranks one step higher than the lowest
          ranking argument.

whereas in (8.49c) and (8.49e), the rhemes, the predicate sacó and the
source de la sala for the former, and the agent don Fermín and the source
de la sala for the latter, are not contiguous in the RSH.
      This observation suggests another possible surface structure con-
straint along the following lines:

   (10.39) A surface structure with two adjacent rhemes is less
           acceptable if they are not contiguous in the RSH than
           if they are.

      In addition to predicting lower acceptability for (8.49c) and (8.49e)
than was predicted by principle (10.38), this new principle predicts that
(8.49d), with three violations of the rhematic hierarchy, is also less
acceptable than predicted by principle (10.38), since its two rhemes,
the agent don Fermín and the patient sus espuelas, are not contiguous in
the RSH because the predicate intervenes between them, according to
principle (5.64). This prediction, which would close the gap between
(8.49d), with three violations, and (8.49a), with four, does not seem
intuitively inadequate, although the complexity of the factors in question makes the validation of such predictions extremely difficult.
      Let us examine, finally, the atypical cases with three rhematic
elements, repeated here for convenience:

   (8.52) a. De la sala don Fermín sacó   sus ESPUELAS.
             Source   Agent   Predicate Patient
             [-rheme]   [+rheme] [+rheme] [+rheme]

          b. Sacó   don Fermín sus espuelas de la SALA.
             Predicate Agent   Patient   Source
             [-rheme] [+rheme]   [+rheme]   [+rheme]

          c. Sus espuelas don Fermín sacó   de la SALA.
             Patient   Agent   Predicate Source
             [-rheme]   [+rheme]   [+rheme] [+rheme]

Although sequence (8.52a) would be considerable more acceptable as
a surface representation of a structure with only sus espuelas as the
rheme, its acceptability as the surface representation of the structure
intended here, i.e. with three rhematic elements, is very low, which is
in perfect accordance with principle (10.38), since this sentence contains three violations of the rhematic hierarchy:
    1) The theme de la sala outranks the rheme don Fermín;
    2) The theme de la sala outranks the rheme sacó;
    3) The theme de la sala outranks the rheme sus espuelas.
As for sentence (8.52b), the rule of RHEME-SPLITTING (8.24) converts
it obligatorily into (10.40).

    (10.40) Don FERMÍN sacó sus espuelas de la SALA.
           'Don FERMÍN took his spurs from the ROOM.'

Finally, the low acceptability of (8.52c) is accounted for by the combined application of principles (10.38) and (10.39). As for the former,
it presents the following violations of the rhematic hierarchy:
    1) The theme sus espuelas outranks the rheme don Fermín;
    2) The theme sus espuelas outranks the rheme sacó.
As for the latter, the rhemes sacó and de la sala are not contiguous
in the RSH.

There is still one class of atypical structures whose behavior is
not entirely accounted for, namely those showing a thematic patient in
pre-rhematic position, like the following:

    (10.41) a. Sus espuelas don Fermín SACÓ de la sala.

          b. Sus espuelas don Fermín sacó de la SALA.

          c. Don Fermín sus espuelas sacó de la SALA.

          d. Don Fermín sus espuelas SACÓ de la sala.

The low acceptability of these sentences is not accounted for by
principle (10.38), since they only contain one violation of the rhematic
hierarchy (the theme sus espuelas outranks the rheme sacó) and, consequently, they should be no more deviant than (10.42),

    (10.42) Don Fermín sacó de la sala sus ESPUELAS.
           'Don Fermín took his SPUES from the room.'

where the theme de la sala outranks the rheme sus espuelas. But quite
clearly, the sentences in (10.41) are less acceptable than (10.42).

If we take the predicate sacó to be rhematic in all four cases, we
could explain the low acceptability of (10.41b) and (10.41c) by reference
to principle (10.39), since the predicate and the source are not contiguous in the RSH. Such an explanation is not available, however, for
the other two cases.

It is important to note that if the predicate in (10.41) is topicalized, they become fully acceptable:

    (10.43) a. Sus espuelas don Fermín las SACÓ de la sala.
             'His spurs, don Fermín TOOK (them) from the room.'

          b. Sus espuelas don Fermín las sacó de la SALA.
             'His spurs don Fermín took from the ROOM.'

          c. Don Fermín sus espuelas las sacó de la SALA.
             'His spurs don Fermín took from the ROOM.'

        d. Don Fermín sus espuelas las SACÓ de la sala.
          'His spurs don Fermín TOOK from the room.'

To explain the difference in acceptability between the sentences in (10.41) and those in (10.43), there are at least the following possibilities:

    a) To require the obligatory application of the rule of TOPIC ASSIGNMENT (9.6) to the patient of sentences like those in (10.41) (recall that rule (9.6) is optional);

    b) To add to the grammar yet another surface structure constraint assigning low acceptability to the sentences in (10.41).

The first solution seems inadequate since it would require 'foresight' in the application of the rule of TOPIC ASSIGNMENT: the rule would apply obligatorily to the patient of a structure which would undergo THEME POSTPOSING in such a way as to generate sequences of the type (10.41). The inclusion of such a powerful device which would allow the grammar to look ahead in the derivation in order to decide whether the rule in question is obligatory or not, is clearly incompatible with the commonly accepted desideratum of constraining the form of the grammar as narrowly as possible. We, consequently, adopt alternative b).

    In order to determine the precise formulation of the surface structure constraint required, let us observe that a sentence like (10.44),

    (10.44) Don Fermín sacó sus espuelas de la SALA.
         'Don Fermín took his spurs from the ROOM.'

which may be interpreted as containing only one rheme, de la sala, and which, consequently, shows a thematic patient in pre-rhematic position, is perfectly acceptable. The crucial difference between this sentence and those in (10.41) is that in (10.44) there is no violation of the rhematic hierarchy.

    Following these observations, the pertinent surface structure constraint may be formulated as follows:

    (10.45) A surface structure is unacceptable if it contains
        a non-topicalized patient which violates the rhem-
        atic hierarchy.

10.3 Postposition of topics

    All the examples of theme postposition considered so far have involved non-topicalized arguments. It may be necessary to point out, then, that a topic may also be postposed. Thus, besides the sentences in (10.43), we have the following:

    (10.46) a. Don Fermín las SACÓ de la sala sus espuelas.
         'Don Fermín TOOK them from the room, his spurs.'

        b. Don Fermín las sacó de la SALA sus espuelas.
         'Don Fermín took them from the ROOM, his spurs.'

        c. Don FERMÍN las sacó de la sala sus espuelas.
         'Don FERMÍN took them from the room, his spurs.'

This type of sentence answers questions like the following:

    (10.47) a. Sus espuelas, ¿qué hizo don Fermín con ellas? (10.46b)[3]
         'His spurs, what did don Fermín do with them?'

        b. Sus espuelas, ¿quién las sacó de la sala? (10.46c)
         'His spurs, who took them from the room?'

This observation does not imply any modification of the rules proposed so far, since the formulation of the rule of THEME POSTPOSING (10.5) is sufficiently general to allow the postposition of any theme, whether topicalized or not. There is, however, one aspect of the postposition of topics which requires further comment. Let us recall that, with the exception of the predicate -- which is obligatorily placed to the immediate right of the rheme by rule (10.13) -- postposed themes may occur in any order. Thus, the following two sentences are completely equivalent:

(10.48) a. Don FERMÍN sacó sus espuelas de la sala.
        b. Don FERMÍN sacó de la sala sus espuelas.
        'Don FERMÍN took his spurs from the room.'

Were this also true of postposed topics, question (10.47b) could be answered not only by (10.46c) but also by (10.49).

(10.49) Don FERMÍN las sacó sus espuelas de la sala.

But this sentence is not as felicitous an answer to (10.47b) as (10.46c). In general, a sentence where the postposed topic occupies the final position sounds better than other variants.

Consider the following additional examples, where the first member of each pair is a more acceptable answer to the pertinent question than the second one:

(10.50) a. MARÍA la cerró con llave la puerta.
        b. MARÍA la cerró la puerta con llave.
        'MARY closed it with a key, the door.'

(10.51) a. ESTEBAN lo perdió en la piscina el anillo.
        b. ESTEBAN lo perdió el anillo en la piscina.
        'STEPHEN lost it in the pool, the ring.'

Just as in the case of pre-rhematic themes, the difference between the a and the b sentences seems to be a matter of style, not grammar. The b sentences are grammatical, although stylistically less acceptable than the a sentences. Consequently, the adequate mechanism to account for this difference is a surface structure constraint, which may be formulated as follows:

(10.52) A surface structure containing a post-rhematic topic is more acceptable if the topic is in final position than if it is not.

A final aspect of the relationship between topics and the rule of THEME POSTPOSING is the following:
If the topic is generic, its postposition does not seem to be permissible, as indicated by examples (10.53) and (10.54).

(10.53) a. Luces naturales no sé si las TENGO.
        b. *No sé si las TENGO luces naturales.
        'Natural lights I don't know if I HAVE them.'

(10.54) a. Dictadores, los hay MUCHOS en nuestra pobre América.
        b. *Los hay MUCHOS en nuestra pobre América, dictadores.
        'Dictators, there are MANY in our poor America.'

Since we know that generic topics may occur without a pronominal copy (see rule (9.28)), it could be argued that sentences like (10.55) contradict the principle just stated.

(10.55) a. No sé si TENGO luces naturales.
              'I don't know if I HAVE natural lights.'

        b. Hay MUCHOS dictadores en nuestra pobre América.
              'There are MANY dictators in our poor America.'

These sentences, however, do not contain topics, but only ordinary postposed themes.

The impossibility of postposing a generic topic is, then, clearly established. Consequently, a condition like the following must be added to the rule of THEME POSTPOSING:

(10.56) THEME POSTPOSING is inapplicable to an element X
        showing the features [+topic, +generic].

10.4 Conclusions

Summing up, emphatic sentences are generated by means of an optional rule of THEME POSTPOSING which includes the following conditions:

(10.5) THEME POSTPOSING (OPTIONAL)

$$
\begin{array}{ccc}
X & + & Y \\
[-\text{rheme}] & & [+\text{rheme}] \\
1 & & 2 \quad \rightarrow \\
\emptyset & & 2 + 1
\end{array}
$$

Conditions:

(10.6) THEME POSTPOSING is applicable only if the sentence is an assertion.

(10.16) If X includes the predicate, it must also include all other elements with the features [-rheme, -topic].

(10.56) THEME POSTPOSING is inapplicable to an element X showing the features [+topic, +generic].

In addition to this general rule, there is a special rule which places a postposed predicate to the immediate right of the rheme:

(10.13) POSTPOSED PREDICATE MOVEMENT (OBLIGATORY)

$$
\begin{array}{cccccc}
X & + & Y & + & Z & \\
[+\text{rheme}] & & [-\text{rheme}] & & \text{Predicate} & \\
& & & & [-\text{rheme}] & \\
1 & & 2 & & 3 & \rightarrow \\
1 + 3 & & 2 & & \emptyset &
\end{array}
$$

Finally, the acceptability of the structures generated by these and the rest of the linear order rules is determined by the following surface structure conditions:

(10.38) The acceptability of a sentence decreases in inverse proportion to the number of violations of the rhematic hierarchy.

(10.39) A surface structure with two adjacent rhemes is less acceptable if they are not contiguous in the RSH than if they are.

(10.45) A surface structure is unacceptable if it contains a non-
topicalized patient which violates the rhematic hierarchy.

(10.52) A surface structure containing a post-rhematic topic is
more acceptable if the topic is in final position than
if it is not.

The interaction between emphatic order, the rhematic hierarchy, and
topicalization is fairly complex, and the rules suggested here do not
pretend to explain it in all its ramifications. The merit of these rules
must be sought not in their exhaustiveness but in their explicitness.

FOOTNOTES TO CHAPTER TEN

[1]The version *Un discurso MARÍA pronunció is disallowed by condition
(10.16), which requires postposition of all non-topical themes when
the predicate is postposed.

[2]These glosses can only be taken as roughly equivalent to the Spanish
sentences, but an examination of structure (8.48) should indicate quite
clearly what the message intended in each case is.

[3]There is no natural question corresponding to (10.46a).

Chapter Eleven

THE ASSIGNMENT OF SENTENTIAL STRESS

The study of sentential stress and intonation is a complex matter which, apart from the pioneering work of Navarro Tomás (1944), has not received much attention in Spanish. Within the American structuralist tradition, the analyses of Stockwell and Bowen (1965) and of Emma Gregores and Jorge A. Suárez in their Spanish version of Hockett's (1958) manual deserve mention as attempts to describe the intonational pattern of standard Spanish, and those of Silva Fuenzalida (1952-3) and Beatriz Fontanella (1966) among those dealing with dialectal variants. None of these studies, however, approaches the problem from the viewpoint of the informational content of the sentence.

In this chapter, we do not presume to analyze the complex phenomenon of Spanish intonation and stress in its entirety. Our aim will be simply the explicit formulation of the rule which we have been referring to as SENTENTIAL STRESS ASSIGNMENT, which plays a crucial role in the identification of the highest ranking rheme.

Let us begin by considering the two-constituent sentences which we have been using throughout this study:

(11.1) a. Empezó la RESISTENCIA.
          'The RESISTANCE started.'

       b. La resistencia EMPEZÓ.
          'The resistance STARTED.'

As we have seen, the first sentence derives from two different rhematic structures: one where both constituents are rhematic, and one where only the patient la resistencia is. On the other hand, sentence (11.1b) derives from only one rhematic structure where the predicate is rhematic. As for the location of the main sentential stress, we note that in both cases it falls on the last rhematic element. The same is true of the emphatic versions of these sentences:

(11.2) a. La RESISTENCIA empezó.
          'The RESISTANCE started.'

       b. EMPEZÓ la resistencia.
          'The resistance STARTED.'

since the predicate and the patient, respectively, are rhematic.

Considering more complex structures, we see that this rule is also applicable to them. Thus, for example, a rhematic structure like the following,

(11.3) $\left\{\begin{array}{llll} \text{sacó,} & \text{don Fermín,} & \text{sus espuelas,} & \text{de la sala} \\ \text{Predicate} & \text{Agent} & \text{Patient} & \text{Source} \\ [\text{+rheme}] & [\text{-rheme}] & [\text{+rheme}] & [\text{+rheme}] \end{array}\right\}$

has the main sentential stress on the source de la sala, since it is this phrase which, being the highest ranking rheme, is placed at the end of the rhematic string by the linear order rules. Thus, according to the rule suggested, whether THEME POSTPOSING applies or not, the location of the sentential stress is always the same for a given rhematic structure:

(11.4) a. Don Fermín sacó sus espuelas de la SALA.
     b. Sacó sus espuelas de la SALA don Fermín.
      'Don Fermín took his spurs from the ROOM.'

Let us consider now what happens when the rule of RHEME SPLITTING, repeated here for convenience, applies:

(8.24) RHEME SPLITTING (OBLIGATORY)

$$\begin{array}{ccc} \text{Predicate} + & X & + & Y \\ [-\text{rheme}] & [+\text{rheme}] & & [+\text{rheme}] \\ 1 & 2 & & 3 \quad \rightarrow \\ 2+1 & \emptyset & & 3 \end{array}$$

This rule applies, for instance, to a structure like (11.5),

(11.5)
$$\left\{ \begin{array}{lll} \text{está procurando,} & \text{ella,} & \text{enseñarte} \\ \text{Predicate} & \text{Agent} & \text{Patient} \\ [-\text{rheme}] & [+\text{rheme}] & [+\text{rheme}] \\ \text{'is trying'} & \text{'she'} & \text{'to teach you'} \end{array} \right\}$$

once the linear order rules have converted it into string (11.6),

(11.6)
$$\begin{array}{lll} \text{está procurando} + & \text{ella} & + & \text{enseñarte} \\ \text{Predicate} & \text{Agent} & & \text{Patient} \\ [-\text{rheme}] & [+\text{rheme}] & & [+\text{rheme}] \end{array}$$

and changes it into (11.7).

(11.7)
$$\begin{array}{lll} \text{ella} & + \text{ está procurando} + & \text{enseñarte} \\ \text{Agent} & \text{Predicate} & \text{Patient} \\ [+\text{rheme}] & [-\text{rheme}] & [+\text{rheme}] \end{array}$$

Now, for this string to be an adequate response to question (11.8),

(11.8) ¿Quién está procurando qué?
      'Who is trying to do what?'

it must have two main sentential stresses, one on the agent ella and one on the patient enseñarte. Since ella is not 'the last rhematic element', the rule suggested above must be modified if we want it to apply to both the agent and the patient.

We notice that the elements which are assigned sentential stress in (11.7) have the following feature in common: neither of them is followed by a rheme; ella is followed by a theme, and enseñarte by a sentence boundary. The following formulation of the rule in question captures this generalization:

(11.9) SENTENTIAL STRESS ASSIGNMENT (OBLIGATORY)

$$\begin{array}{cccc} X & + & Y & + \left\{ \begin{bmatrix} Z \\ [-\text{rheme}] \\ \# \end{bmatrix} \right\} \\ & & [+\text{rheme}] & \\ 1 & & 2 & 3 \quad \rightarrow \\ 1 & & \begin{bmatrix} 2 \\ [+\text{stress}] \end{bmatrix} & 3 \end{array}$$

where # indicates a sentence boundary
and Z is one constituent

This simple rule accounts for all the cases considered in this study, and it seems to be valid for a variety of different dialects. Thus, even though the intonational contours of a Mexican and those of an Argentinian may differ widely, the location of the main sentential stress, which may be signaled by different phonetic devices, seems to be conditioned by the same factors of rhematic structure.

There are, no doubt, many details related to the stress and intonational pattern of Spanish sentences which are relevant to rhematic structure. However, the main aspect of the correlation between rhematic structure and stress is adequately accounted for by the rule suggested here.

Chapter Twelve

NON-RHEMATIC FACTORS AFFECTING LINEAR ORDER

We have so far assumed that linear order is determined solely by
the rhematic structure of the sentence. Important though this factor is,
it is not the only one.

12.1 Length as a possible factor

We could ask ourselves whether length might not be an additional
factor determining linear order. In the case of coordinate structures,
there seems to be a tendency to place longer constituents to the right
of shorter constituents. But this stylistic preference, assuming it
exists, should not be confused with the order imposed by the rhematic
structure of the sentence. In the latter case, as we have seen, there is
a clear distinction between a normal, 'unmarked' order and an emphatic
one. Such a distinction does not exist in the case of coordinate structures. At any rate, the relative order of coordinated elements falls
outside of the scope of this study, since it involves either the internal
order of an immediate constituent of the sentence or the relative order
between two sentences, not the relative order of two immediate constituents of the sentence.

Let us ask, then, if, apart from the case of coordinate structures,
length affects the relative order of the major constituents of the sentence. In the terms of our analysis, this could mean two different
things:

a) long constituents rank higher than short constituents in the
RHEME SELECTION HIERARCHY, which, by the operation of the linear order
rules, would result in rhematic long constituents being assigned final
position over other rhemes; or

b) there is a special linear order rule which places long constituents in final position regardless of their rhematic status.

Alternative b) is easily disproved, for instance, by a sentence like
(12.1),

(12.1) El canto de los insectos, la voz del río, la luz de las
estrellas y el oscuro y profundo cuerpo de las montañas
fortalecían a la joven (Arguedas II.191).
'The singing of the insects, the voice of the rivers, the
light of the stars, and the dark and deep body of the moun-
tains strengthened the young woman.'

with a long non-rhematic constituent in initial position, and by a sentence like (12.2),

(12.2) Mucha sabiduría racional o un orden político estricto funda-
do en los dioses falsos se necesita para dominar esta tierra..
(Arguedas II.11).
'Much rational knowledge or a strict political order based on
false gods is needed in order to master this land...'

with a long rhematic constituent in initial position.

As for alternative a), let us consider a sentence like (12.3).

(12.3) Indios sucios, enflaquecidos, muy pálidos, seguramente ter-
       cianientos, lo vieron pasar con cierta indiferencia (Argue-
       das II.262).
       'Dirty Indians, grown thin, very pale, no doubt feverish, saw
       him pass with a certain indifference.'

The most likely underlying structure for this sentence is one where
all constituents are rhematic. If long rhemes ranked higher than short
rhemes regardless of their underlying category, the normal order of this
sentence would be with the experiencer <u>indios sucios</u>... at the end, but
if the sentence is arranged in that way, it shows all the characteristics
of 'marked' sentences, that is, for instance, it can no longer consist
entirely of new information. Thus, (12.4)

(12.4) Con cierta indiferencia lo vieron pasar indios sucios...

cannot answer a question like (12.5),

(12.5) ¿Qué pasó?
       'What happened?'

but only questions which assume part of the sentence to be given information, for instance, (12.6).

(12.6) ¿Quién lo vio pasar?
       'Who saw him pass?'

It seems, then, that alternative a) must also be rejected.

12.2 Complexity

Another factor which deserves consideration as a possible condition-
er of word order is the relative complexity of sentence constituents.
If we call complex a constituent consisting entirely of a sentence, both
of the following sentences have a complex patient.

(12.7) Creo que va a LLOVER.
       'I think it's going to RAIN.'

(12.8) Me parece que va a LLOVER.
       'It seems to me it's going to RAIN.'

The rheme selection in these sentences appears to be typical, since
in addition to answering questions like (12.9) or (12.10),

(12.9) a. ¿Qué crees?
       b. ¿Qué te parece?
          'What do you think?'

(12.10) Y tú, ¿qué opinas?
        'And you, what do you say?'

they also answer a question like (12.11),

(12.11) ¿Qué hay?
        'What's up?'

that is, all constituents may be considered rhematic, and we know that
for a structure like that LINEAR ORDER II (rule 8.19) places constituents in ascending hierarchical order from left to right. This suggests
that the rhematic hierarchy for these sentences is patient, predicate,
experiencer, which agrees with the general RSH.

This being the case, we cannot tell whether the patient clause is assigned final position because of its high rhematic rank or because of its
internal complexity. In order to determine if complexity has anything to
do with linear order, we must examine cases where the complex constituent
is not rhematic. If such a constituent, contrary to rule (8.4) which
places rhemes after non-rhemes, still tends to go at the end of the sentence, we will have an indication that complexity does play an independent
role in establishing linear order. Let us consider, then, sentences (12.14)
and (12.15).

      (12.14) CREO que va à llover.
           'I THINK it's going to rain.'

      (12.15) Me PARECE que va a llover.
           'It SEEMS to me it's going to rain.'

The derivation of these sentences is roughly like this:
First, the feature $[+\text{rheme}]$ is assigned to the predicate; then
LINEAR ORDER I (rule 8.4) places the predicate in final position by
virtue of its being marked $[+\text{rheme}]$, generating (12.16) and (12.17),

      (12.16) Que va a llover CREO.
           'That it's going to rain I THINK.'

      (12.17) Que va a llover me PARECE.
           'That it's going to rain SEEMS to me.'

which are then optionally converted into (12.14) and (12.15) respectively
by the rule of THEME POSTPOSING (10.5).
    But there is somehing counterintuitive about this derivation. Notice
that in the case of other sentences, for instance, (12.18),

      (12.18) a. Empezó la RESISTENCIA.
           b. La RESISTENCIA empezó.
           'The RESISTANCE started.'

the output of THEME POSTPOSING is more 'marked' than its input, for instance, the former are restricted to assertive contexts whereas the latter
are not. But this is certainly not the case with sentences (12.14) through
(12.17). In fact, it is just the reverse: sentences (12.16) and (12.17)
are more marked than (12.14) and (12.15). This suggests that the 'normal'
position for complex constituents like the patients in (12.14) and (12.15)
is at the end of the sentence regardless of their rhematic status.

12.2.1 The rules

    In order to account for this fact, we propose an obligatory rule,
ordered after LINEAR ORDER I and II (rules 8.4 and 8.19) and before
THEME POSTPOSING (rule 10.5) that places complex constituents in final
position regardless of their rhematic status:

      (12.19) COMPLEX CONSTITUENT POSTPOSING (OBLIGATORY)

$$[X]_S + Y$$
$$1 \qquad 2 \;\rightarrow$$
$$\emptyset \qquad 2 + 1$$

    To see how this rule interacts with the rest of the rules dealing
with linear order, and to provide justification for yet another linear
order rule, let us consider the derivation of rhematic structure (12.20).

(12.20) ⎧creo,   yo,   que va a llover ⎫
        ⎨Predicate Experiencer Patient   ⎬
        ⎪[+rheme]   [-rheme]   [-rheme]   ⎪
        ⎩'believe' 'I'   'it's going to rain'⎭

Linear order rules (8.4) and (8.19) assign to this structure the
following linear order:

(12.21) yo   +   que va a llover + creo
        Experiencer Patient   Predicate
        [-rheme]   [-rheme]   [+rheme]

The rule just proposed, (12.19), converts this sequence into (12.22).

(12.22) yo   +   creo   +   que va a llover
        Experiencer Predicate   Patient
        [-rheme]   [+rheme]   [-rheme]

The rule of THEME POSTPOSING (10.5) may optionally apply to the experiencer _yo_, and string (12.23) may be generated,

(12.23) creo   +   yo   +   que va a llover
        Predicate   Experiencer   Patient
        [+rheme]   [-rheme]   [-rheme]

or the experiencer may be deleted by a rule that does not concern us
here.
     Besides strings (12.22) and (12.23), rhematic structure (12.20) may
have surface representation (12.24),

(12.24) Que va a llover yo CREO.
        'I THINK it's going to rain.'

which is a 'marked' sentence, in the sense that it has less contextual
freedom than the other versions. In order to generate this surface structure, a rule is needed to optionally prepose a complex constituent, along
the lines of (12.25).

(12.25) COMPLEX CONSTITUENT PREPOSING (OPTIONAL)

                 X + [Y]$_S$
                 1   2   →
               2 + 1   ∅

     This rule does for sentences with complex constituents what THEME
POSTPOSING does for other sentences: it produces an 'emphatic' order
which can only be used in assertive environments, that is, when the sentence is either independent or embedded under an assertive verb.
     Notice, for instance, the parallelism between (12.26) and (12.27)
on the one hand,

(12.26) a. CREO que va a llover. (Assertive context)
           'I THINK it's going to rain.'

        b. Digo que CREO que va a llover. (Assertive context)
           'I say I THINK it's going to rain.'

        c. Me alegro de que CREAS que va a llover. (Non-assertive
           context)
           'I'm glad you THINK it's going to rain.'

(12.27) a. Empezó la RESISTENCIA. (Assertive context)
            'The RESISTANCE started.'

        b. Digo que empezó la RESISTENCIA. (Assertive context)
            'I say the RESISTANCE started.'

        c. Me alegro de que empezara la RESISTENCIA. (Non-assertive
            context)
            'I'm glad that the RESISTANCE started.'

and (12.28) and (12.29) on the other.

(12.28) a. Que va a llover CREO. (Assertive context)
            'I THINK it's going to rain.'

        b. Digo que que va a llover CREO. (Assetive context)
            'I say that I THINK it's going to rain.'

        c. *Me alegro de que que va a llover CREAS. (Non-assertive
            context)
            'I'm glad that you THINK it's going to rain.'

(12.29) a. La RESISTENCIA empezó. (Assertive context)
            'The RESISTANCE started.'

        b. Digo que la RESISTENCIA empezó. (Assertive context)
            'I say that the RESISTANCE started.'

        c. *Me alegro de que la RESISTENCIA empezara. (Non-assertive
            context)
            'I'm glad that the RESISTANCE started.'

Consequently, the following condition must be added to rule (12.25):

(12.30) COMPLEX CONSTITUENT PREPOSING applies only if the sentence
         is an assertion.

Let us now see how the rules proposed affect rhematic structure
(12.31).

(12.31) $\left\{ \begin{array}{lll} \text{creo,} & \text{yo,} & \text{que va a llover} \\ \text{Predicate} & \text{Experiencer} & \text{Patient} \\ [\text{-rheme}] & [\text{-rheme}] & [\text{+rheme}] \end{array} \right\}$

Linear rules (8.4) and (8.19) assign the following order to this
structure:

(12.32) yo   +   creo   +   que va a llover
        Experiencer Predicate Patient
        [-rheme]   [-rheme]   [+rheme]

COMPLEX CONSTITUENT POSTPOSING applies vacuously to this structure,
since the complex constituent is already in final position. The derivation
may either end here, or the patient may be preposed, either by the rule
of COMPLEX CONSTITUENT PREPOSING (12.25) or by the application of THEME
POSTPOSING (10.5) to the experiencer and the predicate.

The structure resulting from the application of either one of these
rules is subject to rule (10.13), which places the postposed predicate
to the immediate right of the rheme. The sequence generated is, then, the
following:

(12.33) Que va a LLOVER creo yo.
        'It's going to RAIN, I think.'

Our rules thus accurately predict that the normal order for a structure like (12.21) is as in (12.32), and its emphatic order, as in (12.33).

There is one aspect, however, in the derivation of this last string
which is not quite satisfactory, namely the fact that, although the sentence is not ambiguous, it has two alternative derivations, one through
the application of THEME POSTPOSING and one through the application of
COMPLEX CONSTITUENT PREPOSING. It is possible to prevent this double
derivation by restricting the latter rule to complex constituents which
are thematic: since the patient in (12.32) is rhematic, with this modification the rule of COMPLEX CONSTITUENT PREPOSING does not apply, and
sentence (12.33) derives only by the application of THEME POSTPOSING.

As further support for this modification, let us consider the derivation of a structure where all the constituents are rhematic:

(12.34) $\left\{\begin{array}{lll} \text{creo,} & \text{yo,} & \text{que va a llover} \\ \text{Predicate} & \text{Experiencer} & \text{Patient} \\ [\text{+rheme}] & [\text{+rheme}] & [\text{+rheme}] \end{array}\right\}$

Linear order rule (8.19) converts this structure into the following
string:

(12.35) yo   +   creo +   que va a llover
        Experiencer Predicate Patient
        [+rheme]   [+rheme]   [+rheme]

The rule of COMPLEX CONSTITUENT POSTPOSING applies vacuously to this
string, and the rule of THEME POSTPOSING is inapplicable, since its
structural description is not met. However, the rule of COMPLEX CONSTI-
TUENT PREPOSING -- without the modification we are trying to motivate --
could apply, which would convert this string, after POSTPOSED PREDICATE
MOVEMENT (10.13) and SENTENTIAL STRESS ASSIGNMENT (11.9), into the following structure:

(12.36) Que va a llover creo YO.
        '<u>I</u> think it's going to rain.'

This derivation, however, is clearly inadequate, since sentence
(12.36) does not allow an interpretation where all constituents are
rhematic, but requires that the patient and the predicate be interpreted as themes. The modification proposed avoids this problem.

The revised version of COMPLEX CONSTITUENT PREPOSING is, then, as
follows:

(12.37) COMPLEX CONSTITUENT PREPOSING (OPTIONAL)

$$\begin{array}{ccc} X & + & \left[\begin{array}{c} Y \\ [\text{-rheme}] \end{array}\right]_S \\ 1 & & 2 \qquad \rightarrow \\ 2 + 1 & & \emptyset \end{array}$$

Condition: the sentence is an assertion

12.2.2 Parallelism between THEME POSTPOSING and COMPLEX CONSTITUENT PRE-
       POSING

We stated above that COMPLEX CONSTITUENT PREPOSING has a function
equivalent to that of THEME POSTPOSING: both rules displace an element
from its normal position, thus generating what we have called 'emphatic'

sentences. The parallelism between these two rules is, of course, reflected in their formalization, as can be seen by comparing rule (12.37) with the rule of THEME POSTPOSING, which we repeat here for convenience:

(10.5) THEME POSTPOSING (OPTIONAL)

$$
\begin{array}{cc}
\underset{[-\text{rheme}]}{X} & + & Y \\[6pt]
1 & & 2 \quad \rightarrow \\[6pt]
\emptyset & & 2 + 1
\end{array}
$$

It is clear that these two rules are practically mirror images of each other. Given this parallelism, our theory should allow us to collapse them into one rule, equivalent to the following informal statement:

(12.38) A theme may be optionally displaced, to sentence-initial position if it is a complex element, to sentence-final position otherwise.

Langacker (1968), among others, has proposed a convention for writing mirror-image rules of this type, which consists simply of marking the rule in question with an asterisk. Thus, a rule like (12.39),

(12.39)
$$
\begin{array}{ccccc}
A & + & B & + & C \\
* \; 1 & & 2 & & 3 \quad \rightarrow \\
1 & & \emptyset & & 3 + 2
\end{array}
$$

collapses the following two rules:

(12.40)
$$
\begin{array}{ccccc}
A & + & B & + & C \\
1 & & 2 & & 3 \quad \rightarrow \\
1 & & \emptyset & & 3 + 2
\end{array}
$$

(12.41)
$$
\begin{array}{ccccc}
A & + & B & + & C \\
1 & & 2 & & 3 \quad \rightarrow \\
2 + 1 & & \emptyset & & 3
\end{array}
$$

In our case, there is one more detail: there is a relation of dependency between the 'mirror-image application' of the rule and the complexity of the constituent to be moved. In view of this fact, the following formulation seems appropriate:

(12.42) THEME DISPLACEMENT (OPTIONAL)

$$
\begin{array}{ccccc}
X & + & \left[\underset{[-\text{rheme}]}{Y}\right]_{<S>} & + & Z \\[10pt]
<*> \; 1 & & 2 & & 3 \quad \rightarrow \\[6pt]
1 & & \emptyset & & 3 + 2
\end{array}
$$

Conditions:

a) the sentence is an assertion (=10.6=12.30);

b) if Y includes the predicate, it must also include all the other elements with the features [-rheme, -topic] (=10.16);

c) the rule does not apply to an element Y with the features [+topic, +generic] (=10.56).

The angled brackets around the asterisk and the symbol S must be interpreted as indicating that the rule applies in its mirror-image form only if the symbol S is present, that is, only if the constituent denoted by Y is 'complex'; otherwise, the rule applies in its straight form.

With the formulation of this rule, which captures a significant generalization concerning 'emphatic' order, we close our discussion of the influence of syntactic complexity on linear order.

12.3 Order of non-rhematic adjuncts

The final section in this chapter presents some informal observations on the linear order of certain adjuncts.

Let us recall that, from the viewpoint of rhematic structure, there are two kinds of adjuncts: potential rhemes and non-potential rhemes. The linear distribution of the former is determined by the rules already discussed. Nothing has been said, however, about the linear order of the latter.

The adjuncts which are not potential rhemes have been grouped into five classes:

a) attitude indicators, e.g. <u>francamente</u> 'frankly', <u>por cierto</u> 'of course';

b) sentence relators, e.g. <u>al fin y al cabo</u> 'finally', <u>por lo menos</u> 'at least';

c) topical adjuncts, e.g. <u>técnicamente</u> 'technically', <u>estructural-mente</u> 'structurally';

d) rhematizers, e.g. <u>hasta</u> 'even', <u>casi</u> 'almost';

e) other, e.g. <u>totalmente</u> 'totally', <u>muy</u> 'very'.

We will deal only with the first four classes, since those in the fifth class function only as mediate constituents of the sentence and, consequently, fall outside the scope of this study.

Attitude indicators may appear in any sentence position, as shown by the following examples:

(12.43) a. Me acongoja <u>francamente</u> hablar del asunto.
     b. <u>Francamente</u>, me acongoja hablar del asunto.
     c. Me acongoja hablar del asunto, <u>francamente</u>.
     d. Me acongoja hablar, <u>francamente</u>, del asunto.
       '<u>Frankly</u>, it makes me sad to talk about that matter.'

Sentence relators occur primarily in initial position, as illustrated by the following examples:

(12.44) a. Ya existe un dicho clásico: mal de muchos, consuelo de tontos. <u>Así es que</u> debés pensar en vos mismo, en tu propia responsabilidad (Naranjo 106).
       'There is a classical saying: the sorrow of many is fools' consolation. <u>So</u> you must think of yourself, of your own responsibility.'

     b. Nadie ha chistado. <u>En todo caso</u>, si llegaran a reclamar algo, saben bien que tendría que tomar medidas enérgicas (Naranjo 35).
       'Nobody has complained. <u>In any event</u>, should they complain, they know very well that I would have to take

drastic action.'

    c. Que lo hagan. <u>Al fin y al cabo</u>, eso es lo que quieren esos
       mierdas (Naranjo 51).
       'Let them do it. <u>After all</u>, that is what those shitheads
       want.'

    d. Dejate de lloriqueos, que los hombres no lloran. <u>Por lo</u>
       <u>menos</u> no lo hacen en media calle (Naranjo 105).
       'Stop whimpering; men don't cry. <u>At least</u>, they don't do
       it in the middle of the street.'

but they may also occur in final or internal position:

(12.45) a. Que lo hagan. Eso es lo que quieren esos mierdas, <u>al fin</u>
       <u>y al cabo</u>.
       'Let them do it. That is what those shitheads want, <u>after</u>
       <u>all</u>.'

    b. No tengo capital, no podés heredar de mí más que mi buen
       nombre...Debés <u>entonces</u> hacer tu propio porvenir (Naranjo
       106).
       'I have no money, you can only inherit my good name from
       me...You must <u>then</u> make your own future.'

Topical adjuncts appear in initial position:

(12.46) a. <u>Técnicamente</u>, el problema no tiene solución.
       '<u>Technically</u>, the problem has no solution.'

    b. <u>Estructuralmente</u>, no hay idiomas primitivos.
       '<u>Structurally</u>, there are no primitive languages.'

Rhematizers deserve a more detailed treatment. First, let us recall
that the rheme identified by a rhematizer may be either a whole sentence
or part thereof, as shown, respectively, by the a and the b sentences in
the following pairs:

(12.47) a. --¿Leyó usted los periódicos?
       --<u>Apenas</u> he tenido tiempo de hojearlos (Naranjo 32).
       '--Did you read the newspapers?
       --I have <u>barely</u> had time to browse through them.'

    b. Yo ya no soy nada. Soy <u>apenas</u> la protección que doy a
       mi familia (Naranjo 55).
       'I am no longer anything. I am <u>just</u> the protection which
       I give to my family.'

(12.48) a. Cuando se iba por la calle con él, <u>casi</u> había que correr
       (Naranjo 123).
       'When you walked on the street with him, you <u>almost</u> had
       to run.'

    b. Es <u>casi</u> un niño.
       'He is <u>almost</u> a child.'

(12.49) a. ...tengo detrás de mí una leyenda un poco negra. <u>Hasta</u>
       me llaman terciopelo, por lo peligroso que siempre me
       han encontrado (Naranjo 61).
       '...I have a slightly black legend behind me. They <u>even</u>
       call me velvet, that's how dangerous they've always
       found me.'

b. Lo tengo para todo, <u>hasta</u> para dejar mandados (Naranjo 94).
   'I use it for everything, <u>even</u> to run errands.'

(12.50) a. ...<u>ni siquiera</u> había espacio dónde poner su escritorio
         (Naranjo 60).
         '...there was<u>n't even</u> room for his desk.'

b. El hablar así me demuestra que no tenés <u>ni siquiera</u> una
   idea de lo que se tiene que aguantar en un trabajo...
   (Naranjo 98).
   'Your talking like that shows me that you do<u>n't even</u> have
   the slightest idea about what one must put up with in a
   job...'

(12.51) a. <u>Prácticamente</u> te veía en todos los rostros de mujer y
         todas las voces me parecían la tuya (Naranjo 175).
         '<u>Practically</u> I would see you in every woman's face, and
         every voice sounded like yours.'

b. Recordá que Quesada era <u>prácticamente</u> un hombre feliz
   (Naranjo 123).
   'Remember that Quesada was <u>practically</u> a happy man.'

(12.52) a. Siempre he apreciado mucho a Quesada y <u>precisamente</u> creí
         que sería valioso cerca de la dirección...(Naranjo 120)
         'I have always appreciated Quesada very much and <u>precise-
         ly</u> I thought that he would be useful close to the manage-
         ment.'

b. Ahora vas a salir con obsesiones. <u>Precisamente</u> eso te pasa en el trabajo. ¡Pensás demasiado! (Naranjo 98)
   'Now you are going to start with your obsessions. It is
   <u>precisely</u> that what happens to you at work. You think
   too much!'

(12.53) a. <u>Simplemente</u> quiero expresarle mi solidaridad en esta a-
         marga hora...(Naranjo 126)
         'I <u>just</u> want to express my solidarity with you in this
         bitter hour...'

b. ...eso puede ser <u>simplemente</u> un oficio (Naranjo 134).
   '...that may be <u>just</u> a job.'

(12.54) a. No, <u>solamente</u> le decía lo que pienso hacer (Naranjo 33).
         'No, I was <u>just</u> telling you what I intend to do.'

b. Pensaba <u>solamente</u> en cómo ayudar y servir al prójimo
   (Naranjo 127).
   'I was <u>just</u> thinking of how to aid and serve my fellow
   man.'

(12.55) a. ¡Qué alma tendría yo si <u>sólo</u> pensara en vender y comprar
         cosas..! (Naranjo 96)
         'What kind of a soul would I have if I <u>only</u> thought about
         selling and buying things..!

b. ...en la mañana me dijiste que vendrías <u>sólo</u> a comer (Naranjo 97).
   '...this morning you told me you would come <u>only</u> for din-
   ner.'

(12.56) a. Lo que pasa es que ya casi están enterrando a Quesada (Naranjo 132).
'What happens is that they are already almost burying Quesada.'

b. ...tu ropa ya tiene brillo...(Naranjo 100)
'...your clothes are already beginning to shine...'

In all these examples, the rhematizer occurs right before the rheme. The abundance of examples like these suggests that this is the normal order. We assume, then, that rhematizers are characterized in the lexicon by the contextual feature +[___ [+rheme]. However, a rhematizer may also occur to the right of the rheme, as in the following examples,

(12.57) a. Hay gente que ni sufre, ni goza, que vive nada más (Naranjo 115).
'There are people who neither suffer nor enjoy things, people who just live.'

b. ...es un hombre totalmente embargado entre una plata que entra y otra que sale, sin que alcance casi para lo más necesario (Naranjo 93).
'...he is a man who is completely caught between money that comes in and money that goes out, without its being enough almost for the bare essentials.'

c. Me doy por vencido, no encuentro todavía la forma de hacerte comprender...(Naranjo 114)
'I give up, I can't find the way yet to make you understand...'

or in the middle of the rhematic string, as in these cases:

(12.58) a. Calculo que hemos ya ahorrado una cantidad muy representativa (Naranjo 34).
'I figure we have already saved a very representative amount.'

b. Cuando aceptamos un hueso, vendemos prácticamente el alma al diablo (Naranjo 165).
'When we accept a bone, we practically sell our soul to the devil.'

To account for these cases, we need an optional rule to postpose a rhematizer, along the lines of (12.59).

(12.59) RHEMATIZER POSTPOSING (OPTIONAL)

$$X \quad + \quad Y \quad + \quad Z$$
$$[+rheme]$$

$$1 \qquad 2 \qquad 3 \quad \rightarrow$$

$$\emptyset \qquad 2+1 \qquad 3$$

Condition: X is a rhematizer

Since the variable Y may include the whole or part of the rhematic string, this rule generates both the cases in (12.57) and those in (12.58).

Some rhematizers, like hasta 'even', are exceptions to rule (12.59), and must be marked as such in the lexicon:

(12.60) *Los JEFES hasta se van temprano.
        (Cf. Hasta los JEFES se van temprano.
        'Even BOSSES leave early.')

    Finally, notice that some rhematizers do not precede the rheme directly. Thus, sentence (12.61),

(12.61) Prácticamente te veía en todos los rostros de mujer...
        (Naranjo 175)
        'Practically I would see you in every woman's face...'

in addition to allowing an interpretation where the whole sentence is rhematic, allows one where only the locative constituent en todos los rostros de mujer 'in every woman's face' is. Under this interpretation, of course, the rhematizer prácticamente 'practically' is not directly followed by the rheme. This suggests the need for another optional rule that would prepose a rhematizer to a thematic predicate:

(12.62) RHEMATIZER PREPOSING (OPTIONAL)

    Predicate +   X   +   Y
    [-rheme]   [+rheme]

        1   2   3   →

      2 + 1   ∅   3

        Condition: X is a rhematizer

    That a rhematizer may cross over a thematic predicate and not over other thematic constituents is shown by an example like the following: In sentence (12.63),

(12.63) María le escribió una carta hasta al presidente.
        'Mary wrote a letter even to the president.'

al presidente 'to the president' is interpreted as the rheme; however, if the rhematizer hasta 'even' moves to the left of una carta 'a letter', both una carta and al presidente must be interpreted as rhematic. This contrasts with (12.64),

(12.64) María hasta escribió una carta.
        'Mary even wrote a letter.'

which can be interpreted with either una carta or escribió una carta as rheme.
    This brings us to the end of our comments on the linear order of adjuncts which are not potential rhemes. As we have seen, these elements enjoy in general a considerable degree of freedom of occurrence, and, with the exception of rhematizers, its linear distribution is independent of rhematic structure. In this respect, they contrast with adjuncts which are potential rhemes, whose linear distribution, just like that of other sentential constituents, is determined by the rhematic hierarchy. In other words, the linear distribution of adjuncts which are not potential rhemes is a stylistic matter; that of potentially rhematic adjuncts, a matter of grammar.

12.4 Conclusions

    Summing up, we have considered three matters relative to linear order in this chapter:
    a) the possible influence of the length of constituents;

b) the influence of complexity;
c) the linear order of adjuncts which are not potential rhemes.

With regard to the first question, we have seen that, although there may be a stylistic preference for the postposition of long constituents in coordinate structures, the length of constituents has no influence on the linear order of other structures.

Our analysis of the internal complexity of constituents has shown that it does determine linear order independently of rhematic structure, since the normal order requires a 'complex' constituent to occur at the end of the sentence regardless of its rhematic status. We have also shown a striking parallelism in the two devices which generate emphatic sentences: sentences with a complex thematic constituent allow its displacement to initial position; other sentences allow the displacement of a theme to final position. Conventions generally accepted in transformational grammar allow us to capture this generalization in the form of one optional rule.

Finally, we have seen that among the adjuncts which are not potential rhemes there are two situations with respect to linear order:

a) the normal position of rhematizers is to the immediate left of the rheme, a fact which is expressed in our grammar by assigning to them the lexical feature +[___ [+rheme]. Other positions -- post-rhematic and initial -- result from optional rules;

b) the order of other adjuncts which are not potential rhemes is independent of rhematic structure: topical adjuncts occur in initial position, and the rest anywhere in the sentence.

Chapter Thirteen

THE NOTIONS SUBJECT AND OBJECT

The rules discussed in the preceding chapters deal directly or indirectly with the linear distribution of sentence constituents. Since the application of these rules is based primarily on semantic notions like agent,
patient, instrument, etc. and on 'informational' notions like theme, rheme
and topic, the question arises as to the relevance of syntactic notions
like subject and object for the linear distribution of sentence constituents.

13.1 The notion object

To begin with, we will demonstrate that the category of object is superfluous in a grammar like the one outlined here, with a semantic structure including categories like patient, experiencer, beneficiary, etc.
One of the purposes of identifying a noun phrase as 'direct object'
is to be able to formulate a rule of passivization which, among other
things, 'places the direct object in initial position.' But this rule is
more adequately formulated if we substitute the semantic category patient
for the syntactic category direct object. We know that passivization does
not apply to the 'direct objects' underlined in the following sentences:

(13.1) a. Este collar vale una fortuna.
        'This necklace is worth a fortune.'

      b. El general pesa doscientos kilos.
        'The general weighs two hundred kilos.'

The mechanism usually proposed for preventing this rule from applying
to such sentences is marking the verbs valer 'to be worth' and pesar 'to
weigh' in the lexicon as exceptions to the rule of passivization or, alternatively, as incompatible with a PASSIVE formative which triggers the
passivization rule. But this solution, of course, fails in the case of pesar, since a sentence like the following may undergo passivization:

(13.2) El general pesa los sacos del correo.
        'The general weighs the mail bags.'

In terms of semantic categories, this problem has a straightforward
solution: the verb pesar 'to weigh' is compatible both with complements
like doscientos kilos 'two hundred kilos' and with patients like los sacos
del correo 'the mail bags', and only patients are affected by passivization; the verb valer 'to be worth', on the other hand, only takes complements, so it never occurs in a passive form.
This formulation of the rule of passivization also casts some doubts
on the need for a distinction between a 'direct' and an 'indirect' object,
since one of the arguments for it is that in Spanish only the former becomes the subject of a passive sentence.
Another argument in favor of the distinction between direct and indirect objects is the formal difference between the third person 'accusative'
pronouns la and lo, on the one hand, and the 'dative' pronoun le on the
other. But this formal difference does not correspond to direct and indirect object in all dialects. Thus, in the so-called leísta dialects, le is
used when the antecedent is human, regardless of its syntactic function.
In a grammar like ours, this dialectal variation does not constitute a

serious anomaly, since the basis for distinguishing between these pronominal forms is semantic to begin with, and it may, consequently, be expected
of dialects to differ in their choice of controlling semantic features.
For the theory which predicts the difference in terms of surface syntactic
categories like direct and indirect object, on the other hand, leísta dialects represent a completely unexpected type of irregularity.

Finally, the category of indirect object is insufficient to account
for certain cases of ambiguity like the one shown in (13.3),

> (13.3) Le compré un libro a Pedro.
> 'I bought a book for Peter.'
> or
> 'I bought a book from Peter.'

where a Pedro may be either a beneficiary or a source. To say that in the
first case we have a 'complemento circunstancial' is simply to give an un-
motivated label to an unexplained phenomenon.

This last example, besides showing the inadequacy of the traditional
explanation, also reveals the failure of Chomsky's (1965) 'configurational' definition of functional notions when applied beyond 'subject' and 'object'. If an object is to be characterized as the noun phrase dominated by
a verb phrase, how is the distinction between direct and indirect object
to be characterized? Or the distinction between indirect object and 'complemento circunstancial'? None of the alternatives within Chomsky's theory
is very appealing.

If the indirect object, like the direct object, is a deep structure
noun phrase, since they are both dominated by the verb phrase we are o-
bliged to define their difference in terms of position, which, apart from
forcing us into an arbitrary decision regarding which object comes first
in deep structure, does not seem to be in agreement with the spirit of the
definition of functional notions which is in terms of dominance, not in
terms of linear order.

If, on the other hand, the indirect object is distinguished from the
direct object by its being a deep-structure prepositional phrase, how is
the indirect object to be differentiated from the 'complemento circunstancial', which is also a prepositional phrase? We will be forced again into
distinguishing between functional notions on the basis of an arbitrarily
established linear order. The problems created by a grammar of this sort,
which does not distinguish between different kinds of prepositional phrases
in deep structure, have been adequately examined by Fillmore (1968), and
need not be explored further.

We conclude that the traditional notions direct object, indirect object and complemento circunstancial are superfluous in a grammar which recognizes semantic categories like patient, experiencer, source, beneficiary, etc. We conclude, furthermore, that the characterization proposed for
these notions in classical transformational grammar is untenable.

13.2 The notion subject

Let us now consider the notion subject. To begin with, we must distinguish between underlying and surface subject. The underlying subject of
(13.4) is los militares 'the military'; its surface subject, Víctor Jara,

> (13.4) Víctor Jara fue asesinado por los militares.
> 'Víctor Jara was murdered by the military.'

Fillmore (1968) has demonstrated convincingly that the notion of underlying subject is superfluous in a grammar which includes semantic no-

tions like agent, experiencer, patient, etc.

As for the surface subject, we will pose the following questions:

a) Is its existence motivated?; and (anticipating a positive answer to this question)

b) What is its formal characterization?

The positive answer to question a) is based on the existence of several transformational rules which require the identification of an argument as subject, for instance, the rules of SUBJECT RAISING, EQUIVALENT NOUN PHRASE DELETION, and SUBJECT-VERB AGREEMENT.

We will illustrate the first two of these rules as they are formulated in standard transformational grammar, since this is the only explicit formulation available. The reformulation which would be required within the theory proposed here would not affect the purpose of the illustration, which is only to show the need to identify one element as subject.

The rule of SUBJECT RAISING changes a structure like (13.5) into (13.6),

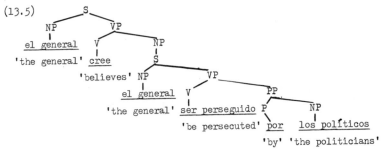

(13.5)

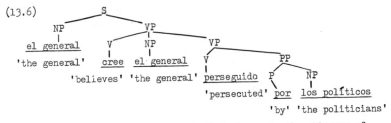

(13.6)

that is, it raises the subject of the embedded clause to the category of constituent of the higher sentence. This structure, after the application of REFLEXIVIZATION, becomes sentence (13.7).

(13.7) El general se cree perseguido por los políticos.
'The general believes himself to be persecuted by the politicians.'

The rule of EQUIVALENT NOUN PHRASE DELETION would also apply optionally to a structure like (13.5), and convert it into (13.8).

(13.8)

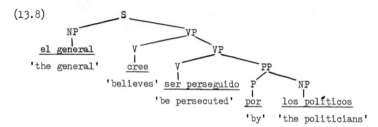

It is clear from these two rules that one argument must be identified as subject.

As for the formal characterization of the subject, there are two possibilities:

a) the subject is identified by its position within the phrase marker;

b) the subject is marked by a feature [+subject].

A priori, the first alternative would seem preferable, since the unlimited proliferation of features might confer excessive power to the grammar. However, we will see that in this case, the criteria of simplicity and descriptive adequacy favor the second alternative.

Within a grammatical theory similar to the one proposed in this study, Fillmore (1968) has formulated a rule which identifies the subject according to criterion a). Starting from a structure like (13.9), for example,

(13.9)
```
              S
         /        \
    Modality    Proposition
              /      \
         Predicate Agent Patient
```

the rule of SUBJECT FORMATION -- on the basis of a hierarchy where the agent outranks the patient -- generates a structure like (13.10),

(13.10)
```
                 S
          /      |      \
    Modality  Agent  Proposition
                     /     \
                Predicate Patient
```

that is, it 'extracts' the agent from the proposition and promotes it to immediate constituent of the sentence. The identification of the subject required by the rules mentioned above is, then, done by reference to the NP directly dominated by S, or, from the linear point of view, by reference to the NP directly preceding the predicate.

Let us see what this treatment of the subject implies. In the case of structures like (13.11), with only one argument,

(13.11) { empezó,   la resistencia }
         { Predicate Patient   }
         { 'started' 'the resistance'}

this argument is promoted to the pre-verbal position, and sentence (13.12) is generated.

(13.12) La resistencia empezó.
        'The resistance started.'

In order to generate sentence (13.13),

(13.13) Empezó la resistencia.

a SUBJECT-PREDICATE INVERSION rule must be posited.

But his analysis contradicts our intuitions with respect to this type of sentence. As we have repeatedly shown in the preceding chapters, the basic, unmarked order is that of sentence (13.13). According to this analysis, however, sentence (13.13) is characterized as less basic than (13.12) since it requires one more rule.

This analysis introduces an artificial difference between sentences like (13.14) and (13.15).

(13.14) Creo que va a llover.
        'I think it's going to rain.'

(13.15) Me parece que va a llover.
        'It seems to me that it's going to rain.'

The complement clause in the first sentence does not undergo any movement rules; that of the second, however, must be first promoted to 'subject' position and then returned to final position by some SUBJECT-PREDICATE INVERSION rule.

The linear order of the second sentence is thus characterized as less basic than that of the first and, of course, as less basic than that of sentence (13.16).

(13.16) Que va a llover me parece.
        'That it's going to rain seems to me.'

Both of these characterizations are clearly counterintuitive.

The positional (or configurational) analysis of the subject is also inadequate with respect to the rule of SUBJECT-VERB AGREEMENT.

To begin with, it is suspicious, as noted by Staal (1967:14), to formulate the rule of agreement in linear terms ('the verb agrees with the preceding NP') when the phenomenon of agreement itself has nothing to do with linear order. But there are other more specific difficulties.

It is well known that in some Spanish equational sentences like the ones in (13.17), the verb agrees not with the 'subject' but with the predicate nominal.

(13.17) a. El problema {eres / *es} TÚ.
           'The problem is YOU.'

        b. El problema {son / *es} los MILITARES
           'The problem is the MILITARY.'

A theory requiring the agreement of the verb with the preceding NP has two alternatives with respect to this type of sentence:
a) to derive them from structures where the surface predicate nominal is in pre-verbal, that is, 'subject', position;
b) to mark them as exceptions to the general rule of agreement, and to formulate an ad-hoc rule of agreement between the verb and the predicate nominal just for these cases.

The first alternative fails for the following reasons:
These sentences cannot be derived from structures like those in (13.18)

(13.18) a. TÚ eres el problema.
           'YOU are the problem.'

b. Los MILITARES son el problema.
   'The MILITARY is the problem.'

without falling into the absurdity of treating emphatic sentences as basic
and normal sentences as marked. To derive them from the sentences in (13.19)

(13.19) a. Tú eres el PROBLEMA.
        'You are the PROBLEM.'

        b. Los militares son el PROBLEMA.'
           'The military are the PROBLEM.'

is also unacceptable, since they are not semantically equivalent: whereas
the sentences in (13.17) answer question (13.20),

(13.20) ¿Quién es el problema?
        'Who is the problem?'

those in (13.19) answer questions like these:

(13.21) a. ¿Qué soy yo?
        'What am I?'

        b. ¿Qué son los militares?
           'What are the military?'

The second alternative requires an arbitrary and counterintuitive
formulation. But let us first see what factors determine agreement in the
cases under consideration.

In sentence (13.17a), there is a difference in the category of person
between the subject and the predicate nominal, and the verb agrees with
the second, rather than with the third, person. If instead of second and
third the equational sentence included first and third person, the verb
would agree with the first person pronoun:

(13.22) El problema $\begin{Bmatrix} soy \\ *es \end{Bmatrix}$ yo.
        'The problem is me.'

If, on the other hand, the sentence includes first and second person,
the verb agrees with whichever person appears in the subject position:

(13.23) a. Yo $\begin{Bmatrix} soy \\ *eres \end{Bmatrix}$ tú.
        'I am you.'

        b. Tú $\begin{Bmatrix} eres \\ *soy \end{Bmatrix}$ yo.

           'You are me.'

To account for these facts, the theory under consideration would have
to include the following elements:
   a) a general rule of agreement which applies, among other cases, to
the sentences in (13.23), and which makes the verb agree with the preceding
NP;
   b) some device to mark sentences like those in (13.17) and (13.22) as
exceptions to that rule;
   c) an ad-hoc rule of agreement which applies to sentences like those
in (13.17) and (13.22).
   As for the general rule, we have already commented on the oddity of a
rule which assigns agreement on the basis of linear arrangement.
   Let us now ask what form the device mentioned in b) might have. It is

clear that the exceptional character in question is that of the sentence
as a whole, not that of an individual constituent. Consequently, this type
of irregularity cannot be accounted for by means of lexical features, as
suggested by Lakoff (1965), but as a specific condition making the rule of
agreement inapplicable to sentences showing the following features:
  a) the verb is <u>ser</u> 'to be';
  b) one NP is third person, and the other first or second.
The ad-hoc character of this set of conditions should be clear.
    Finally, this theory must include a special rule of agreement which
makes the verb agree with the first or second person pronoun regardless of
linear order.
    Sentence (13.17b) shows that the situation is even more complex, since
equational sentences where the NP's differ in number must also be excluded
from the domain of the general rule of agreement, and an additional ad-hoc
rule must be added to make the verb agree with the plural NP in these
cases.
    The alternative which identifies the subject by means of a feature --
also suggested by Goldin (1968) -- has clear advantages over the positional theory.
    Let us formulate the rule in question as follows:

  (13.24) SUBJECT SELECTION (OBLIGATORY)

        Assign the feature [+subject],

        a) in a structure with a patient and an identifier,

            (i) if one argument is [+third person] and the other
                [-third person], to the latter;

            (ii) if they differ in number, to the argument marked
                 [+plural];

        b) in other structures, to the highest ranking argument in
           the following hierarchy: agent, instrument, experiencer,
           patient, identifier.

    This formulation allows us to simplify the rule of agreement to the
following:

  (13.25) The verb agrees in person and number with the argument having
          the feature [+subject].

    The 'subject' identified by rule (13.24) does not always correspond,
of course, to the traditional subject, but is simply the argument with
which the verb agrees.
    Let us compare this analysis with the one discussed above. First, this
analysis does not require any exception features. Second, there is no counterintuitive treatment of agreement in terms of linear order. Third, the
treatment of agreement is unified, not split into two or three unrelated
rules. Finally, since our analysis divorces agreement from linear order
entirely, it reflects accurately the fundamental difference between the
rule of agreement and other rules like TOPIC PLACEMENT or THEME DISPLACE-
MENT, which are clearly linear order rules.
    To close this chapter, let us consider still some other 'special'
cases of agreement:

  (13.26) a. Llovió monedas del cielo.
          b. Llovieron monedas del cielo.
             'It rained coins from the sky.'

(13.27) a. Había muchas personas en la fiesta.
        b. Habían muchas personas en la fiesta (non-standard).
           'There were many people at the party.'

   The positional theory of subject formation requires the optional pro-
motion of the patients to subject position in order to generate the b sentences, followed by the now obligatory application of the rule of SUBJECT-
PREDICATE INVERSION, which suggests erroneously that the linear arrangement
of such sentences is less basic than that of the a sentences. Within the
theory proposed here, a lexical feature of _llover_ 'to rain' and _haber_ 'there
to be, exist' allows the optional assignment of the feature [+subject] to
the patient. This type of specification is needed independently for verbs
like _gustar_ 'to like', which allow either the experiencer or the patient
to function as subject, as shown by the two variants in (13.28),

   (13.28) a. Gusto de la música.
              'I like music.'

           b. Me gusta la música.
              'Music is pleasing to me.'

so its use for verbs like _llover_ and _haber_ does not constitute a great com-
plication of the grammar.

13.3 Conclusions

   Summing up, we have demonstrated that the categories _direct object_,
indirect object and _complemento circunstancial_ are superfluous within the
theory proposed here.
   As for the notion _subject_, we accept Fillmore's arguments to the effect that this category is irrelevant in deep structure.
   Finally, we have demonstrated that the specification of surface structure subjects by means of a feature makes it possible to formulate a sim-
pler and more coherent rule of agreement than its identification by position. This solution, furthermore, explicitly recognizes that the only reason
an argument must be identified as subject is so the verb may agree with it.

Chapter Fourteen

IMPLICATIONS FOR SENTENCES WITH INDETERMINATE 'SUBJECTS'

The analysis of indeterminate-subject sentences like (14.1) and (14.2)

(14.1) Se vende flores.
    'Flowers are sold.'

(14.2) Se venden flores.
    'Flowers are sold.'

has been the topic of numerous articles. While some grammarians analyze
these sentences as representing the same underlying structure -- a view
which I subscribe to -- others derive (14.2) from a 'passive' structure
which also underlies a sentence like (14.3),

(14.3) Las flores se venden.
    'The flowers are for sale.'

and there is even a study (Otero 1972) that denies grammaticality to a sentence like (14.2).

It is my belief that much of the debate concerning constructions of
this type is rendered worthless through a lack of attention to rhematic
structure, topicalization and stress pattern, factors which in my view are
crucial to an understanding of these sentences.

Rather than examining the different claims which have been made in relation to indeterminate-subject sentences, I will show directly how the
rules discussed in the preceding chapters affect them, and leave to the
reader the task of comparing the analysis thus arrived at with other alternatives.[1]

In terms of our analysis, semantic structure (14.4)

(14.4) { vender,   flores,   INDETERMINATE }
       { Predicate Patient   Agent }
       { 'sell'   'flowers' }

is the source of sentences (14.1) through (14.3).

The application of RHEME ASSIGNMENT and TOPIC ASSIGNMENT may convert
this structure into the following rhematic structures:

(14.5) (vender,   flores,   INDETERMINATE)
       Predicate Patient   Agent
       [-rheme] [+rheme] [-rheme]
       [-topic]

(14.6) (vender,   flores,   INDETERMINATE)
       Predicate Patient   Agent
       [+rheme] [+rheme] [-rheme]

(14.7) (vender,   flores,   INDETERMINATE)
       Predicate Patient   Agent
       [+rheme] [-rheme] [-rheme]
             [+topic]

(14.8) (vender,   flores,   INDETERMINATE)[2]
       Predicate Patient   Agent
       [+rheme] [-rheme] [-rheme]
              [-topic]

Let us now determine which structures underlie which sentences.

Beginning with (14.1), we notice that this sentence can answer either question (14.9) or (14.10).

(14.9) ¿Qué se vende?
'What is being sold?'

(14.10) ¿Qué pasa?
'What's up?'

This means that sentence (14.1) has both (14.5) and (14.6) as underlying structures.

What about (14.2)? It also answers questions (14.9) and (14.10), so it must be derived from the same underlying structures.

But how is the formal difference between (14.1) and (14.2) to be accounted for? Since the difference between these two sentences has to do with agreement, the answer to this question must be sought in the rule which selects one argument as 'subject'. Let us recall the formulation of that rule:

(13.24) SUBJECT SELECTION (OBLIGATORY)

Assign the feature [+subject],

a) in a structure with a patient and an identifier,

(i) if one argument is [+third person] and the other [-third person], to the latter;

(ii) if they differ in number, to the argument marked [+plural];

b) in other structures, to the highest ranking argument in the following hierarchy: agent, instrument, experiencer, patient, identifier.

To account for the different agreement in (14.1) and (14.2), all that is needed is the following addition to the rule of SUBJECT SELECTION:

(14.11) The subject-selection hierarchy may be optionally altered when the highest ranking argument is indeterminate.

This addition makes it possible to assign the feature [+subject] either to the agent or to the patient in the rhematic structures considered above, which results in two different applications of the rule of agreement.

As for the order of sentences (14.1) and (14.2), it is determined by the linear order rules presented in the preceding chapters. In the case of rhematic structure (14.5), rule (8.4) places the rheme _flores_ 'flowers' to the right of the other constituents, and rule (8.19), in conjunction with the RSH, places the predicate to the right of the agent. The same linear order results from rhematic structure (14.6), whose rhemes _vender_ 'to sell' and _flores_ 'flowers' are placed to right of the indeterminate agent by rule (8.4), and then ordered with respect to each other according to rhematic rank by rule (8.19). In both cases, the main sentential stress is assigned to the patient _flores_ by rule (11.9).

Let us now consider rhematic structure (14.7). The linear order rules convert it into (14.12),

(14.12) INDETERMINATE + flores   + vender
        Agent   Patient   Predicate
        [-rheme]   [-rheme]   [+rheme]
                      [+topic]

which TOPIC PLACEMENT (9.12) converts into (14.13).

(14.13) flores   # INDETERMINATE + flores   + vender
        Patient   Agent   Patient   Predicate
        [-rheme] [-rheme]   [-rheme]   [+rheme]
        [+topic]   [+topic]
                             [+pro]

I will contend that this structure underlies both (14.3) and (14.14),

(14.14) Las flores se las VENDE.
        'The flowers are for SALE.'

assuming that the topic has the feature [-generic]; with the opposite value
for this feature, sentences like (14.15) are generated.

(14.15) Flores se VENDEN (lo que no se vende {es \ VENDURAS).
                                    {son}
        'Flowers SELL (what doesn't sell is VEGETABLES).'

Let me explain first how (14.3) and (14.14) are generated.
As for the clitic se, we will assume that its insertion is triggered
by the presence of an indeterminate argument, which is obligatorily deleted.[3]
Since the SUBJECT SELECTION rule allows two possibilities in this
case (see 14.11), let us assume first that the feature [+subject] is assigned to the patient flores. With this subject selection, the rule of
agreement assigns to the predicate the features [+third person, +plural],
after which all that is needed for structure (14.13) to become sentence
(14.3) is the deletion of the 'subject' pronoun. There is ample justification for such a rule in Spanish, as shown, for instance, by the following
variants:

(14.16) a. Tú no conoces a María.
       b. No conoces a María.
         'You don't know Mary.'

Since this is an optional rule, the following sentence may also be
derived from (14.13):

(14.17) Las flores, ellas se VENDEN.
        'The flowers, they are for SALE.'

which at least in some dialects is a perfectly acceptable variant.[4]
Let us assume now that the feature [+subject] is assigned to the indeterminate agent. In this case, the verb acquires the features [+third person, -plural], and the pronominal form of the patient flores is las, as a
result of a rule of CASE MARKING which takes into account the 'non-subject'
character of this pronoun. After the insertion of the clitic se and the deletion of the indeterminate agent, sentence (14.14) is generated.
Our rules correctly rule out structures like the following:

(14.18) *Las flores se las VENDEN.[5]

(14.19) *Las flores se VENDE.

In the first one, the verb inflection indicates that the patient flores has the feature [+subject], whereas the form las of its pronominal co-

py indicates the opposite.

As for (14.19), it is also impossible to derive it from a structure with a topicalized patient, since the pronominal copy of the topic can only be deleted when it has the feature [+subject], and the verb inflection indicates that that feature has been assigned to the agent.

Our rules, however, do allow the derivation of (14.19) from a structure without a topic. Whether this is desirable or not is not clear. An indication that it might be correct for the grammar to generate such a sentence comes from the fact that its acceptability seems to increase with the application of THEME POSTPOSING:

(14.20) Se VENDE, las flores.

This is a problem which requires further examination, however.

Let us now consider the possible derivations of (14.12) when the patient _flores_ has the feature [+generic].

TOPIC PLACEMENT (9.12) generates a structure just like (14.13) but with the feature [+generic] attached to the patient. Depending on whether the indeterminate agent or the [+pro] patient is assigned the feature [+subject], either (14.21) or (14.22) is generated,

(14.21) Flores, se las VENDE.
        'As for flowers, you SELL them.'

(14.22) Flores, (ellas) se VENDEN.
        'Flowers are SOLD.'

after AGREEMENT, CASE MARKING, SUBJECT PRONOUN DELETION, and INDETERMINATE ARGUMENT DELETION.

So far, the derivation of these sentences with a [+generic] patient proceeds just like that of the [-generic] counterparts. However, there is one more possibility with a [+generic] patient. Let us recall that in order to explain the free variation in sentences like the following,

(14.23) a. Luces naturales no sé si las tengo.
       b. Luces naturales no sé si tengo.
         'Natural lights, I don't know if I have (them).'

we proposed a rule (9.28) that deletes a topical generic pronoun optionally. If we apply this rule to the structure from which we have derived (14.21) and (14.22), the following sentence will also be generated:

(14.24) Flores, se VENDE.

which is quite acceptable in the same contexts as (14.21), for instance, (14.25).

(14.25) Flores, se VENDE; lo que no se vende $\begin{Bmatrix} es \\ son \end{Bmatrix}$ verduras.
        'Flowers SELL; what doesn't sell is vegetables.'

Let us now consider structure (14.8), repeated here for convenience.

(14.8) $\left\{ \begin{matrix} \text{vender,} & \text{flores,} & \text{INDETERMINATE} \\ \text{Predicate} & \text{Patient} & \text{Agent} \\ [\text{+rheme}] & \begin{bmatrix} \text{-rheme} \\ \text{-topic} \end{bmatrix} & [\text{-rheme}] \end{matrix} \right\}$

The combined effect of LINEAR ORDER I (8.4) and LINEAR ORDER II (8.19) on this structure is shown in (14.26).

(14.26) INDETERMINATE + flores   +   vender
        Agent   Patient   Predicate
        [-rheme]   [-rheme]   [+rheme]
                           [-topic]

Restricting ourselves to the case where the patient is [-generic], from this structure both (14.3) and (14.19) would be generated.

(14.3) Las flores se VENDEN.
        'The flowers are for SALE.'

(14.19) ?Las flores se VENDE.

We have already noted the problematic character of the latter, and there is nothing to be added here.

Let us now consider the effects of THEME POSTPOSING (10.5) on the structures under discussion.

We begin with structure (14.5), repeated here for convenience.

(14.5) { vender,   flores,   INDETERMINATE }
        Predicate Patient   Agent
        [-rheme]   [+rheme]   [-rheme]
        [-topic]

After this structure has been converted into (14.27)

(14.27) INDETERMINATE + vender   + flores
        Agent   Predicate   Patient
        [-rheme]   [-rheme]   [+rheme]
                         [-topic]

by the linear order rules, THEME POSTPOSING (10.5) converts it into (14.28),

(14.28) flores   + INDETERMINATE + vender
        Patient   Agent   Predicate
        [+rheme]   [-rheme]   [-rheme]
                                      [-topic]

which, depending on the application of SUBJECT SELECTION, and after AGREE-MENT, will become either (14.29) or (14.30).

(14.29) FLORES se vende.
        'FLOWERS are sold.'

(14.30) FLORES se venden.
        'FLOWERS are sold.'

As for the remaining structures introduced at the beginning of this chapter, (14.6), with both relevant constituents being rhematic, does not meet the structural description of THEME POSTPOSING. Let us see, however, how THEME POSTPOSING affects the other two structures, beginning with (14.7), repeated here for convenience.

(14.7) { vender,   flores,   INDETERMINATE }
        Predicate Patient   Agent
        [+rheme]   [-rheme]   [-rheme]
                   [+topic]

The linear order rules convert this structure into (14.12), repeated here,

(14.12) INDETERMINATE + flores   + vender
        Agent   Patient   Predicate
        [-rheme]   ⎡-rheme⎤   [+rheme]
                           ⎣+topic⎦

which, as we have seen, will become (14.13) after TOPIC PLACEMENT.

(14.13) flores   # INDETERMINATE + flores   + vender
        Patient   Agent   Patient   Predicate
        ⎡-rheme⎤   [-rheme]   ⎡-rheme⎤   [+rheme]
        ⎣+topic⎦   ⎢+topic⎥
                                     ⎣+pro ⎦

THEME POSTPOSING (10.5) will optionally change this structure into
(14.31),

(14.31) vender   + INDETERMINATE + flores   # flores
        Predicate   Agent   Patient   Patient
        [+rheme]   [-rheme]   ⎡-rheme⎤   ⎡-rheme⎤
                                       ⎢+topic⎥   ⎣+topic⎦
                                       ⎣+pro ⎦

which, depending on the application of SUBJECT SELECTION, will generate
either (14.32) or (14.33),

(14.32) Se las VENDE, las flores.
        'They are for SALE, the flowers.'

(14.33) (Ellas) se VENDEN, las flores.
        'They are for SALE, the flowers.'

assuming that the patient is [-generic].
    If the topic is [+generic], THEME POSTPOSING does not apply, since
there is a specific condition (10.56), independently motivated, which does
not allow it. This condition, formulated to prevent the optional transformation of (14.34) into the ungrammatical string (14.35),

(14.34) Luces naturales no sé si las TENGO.
        'Natural lights I don't know if I HAVE (them).'

(14.35) *No sé si las TENGO, luces naturales.
        'I don't know if I HAVE them, natural lights.'

has the effect of preventing the transformation of the sentences in (14.36)
into those in (14.37),

(14.36) a. Flores, se las VENDE.
        b. Flores, (ellas) se VENDEN.
        c. ?Flores se VENDE.

(14.37) a. *Se las VENDE, flores.
        b. *(Ellas) se VENDEN, flores.
        c. *Se VENDE, flores.

which is strong confirmation for the rules proposed, since none of the sentences in (14.37) is grammatical.
    Finally, let us consider the effect of THEME POSTPOSING on structure
(14.8), repeated here.

(14.8) ⎧ vender,   flores,   INDETERMINATE ⎫
       ⎪ Predicate   Patient   Agent   ⎪
       ⎨ [+rheme]   ⎡-rheme⎤   [-rheme]   ⎬
       ⎪   ⎣-topic⎦   ⎪
       ⎩   ⎭

One of the sentences generated from this structure is (14.3),

(14.3) Las flores se VENDEN.
      'The flowers are for SALE.'

which THEME POSTPOSING optionally converts into (14.38).

(14.38) Se VENDEN las flores.

We have already commented on the fact that our rules also derive apparently ungrammatical (14.39),

(14.39) ?Las flores se VENDE.

which, however, becomes more acceptable after THEME POSTPOSING has applied:

(14.40) ?Se VENDE las flores.

I have nothing to add about these sentences here.
Finally, from a structure containing a generic patient, sentences (14.22) and (14.24) are generated,

(14.22) Flores se VENDEN.

(14.24) Flores se VENDE.

which are turned into (14.41) and (14.42) respectively by THEME POSTPOSING.

(14.41) Se VENDEN flores.

(14.42) Se VENDE flores.

This concludes our discussion of sentences with indeterminate arguments. We have demonstrated that the rules proposed in the preceding chapters, plus some rules which have not been discussed in detail but which are amply justified, e.g. deletion of the indeterminate argument, deletion of the subject pronoun, case marking, allow us to account for a variety of surface representations for this type of structure in an intuitively satisfying manner.

FOOTNOTES TO CHAPTER FOURTEEN

[1] Contreras 1974 contains a discussion of different analyses of these sentences. I no longer subscribe, however, to the solution favored there, for reasons which should be obvious to any reader of this book.

[2] Indeterminate arguments cannot be rhemes or topics. I do not consider here the structure where the predicate is selected as topic: En cuanto a vender, se vende(n) flores 'As for selling, flowers are sold.'

[3] More precisely, the insertion of se occurs when there is a low ranking indeterminate argument in the sentence. Thus, for instance, semantic structure (i)

(i) { vender,   flores,   Juan,   INDETERMINATE }
    { Predicate   Patient   Agent   Target   }

does not underlie a string like (ii),

(ii) *Juan se vendió las flores.

but only strings like (iii) and (iv),

(iii) Juan vendió las FLORES.
      'John sold the FLOWERS.'
(iv) Las flores las vendió JUAN.
     'JOHN sold the flowers.'

because the indeterminate target ranks high in the RSH.

[4] There are other dialects where 'subject' pronouns must be obligatorily deleted when the antecedent is inanimate.

[5] This sentence is grammatical, but not in the sense intended here, that is, as a surface representation of structure (14.7).

CONCLUSIONS

In this study, I have shown that sentences which are normally considered stylistic variants of each other are not equivalent either semantically or syntactically, but they differ in choice and/or location of rheme or topic.

After demonstrating that the rhematic structure of the sentence has semantic and syntactic import, I have proposed some tentative rules governing the selection of rhemes and topics and their linear arrangement, as well as the assignment of the main sentential stress. These rules, in particular, account for the informal distinctions between typical and atypical rheme selection on the one hand, and normal and emphatic order on the other. They also account for some rather intricate relationships between rhematic structure and topicalization.

The main rules proposed are RHEME ASSIGNMENT, TOPIC ASSIGNMENT, LINEAR ORDER I and II, TOPIC PLACEMENT, THEME POSTPOSING and SENTENTIAL STRESS ASSIGNMENT.

The first two assign the features [+rheme] and [+topic] respectively to any sentence constituent. Whether rheme assignment is typical or not is determined by reference to a RHEME SELECTION HIERARCHY, which ranks the different arguments and adjuncts according to their relative propensity to be used as rhemes. LINEAR ORDER I places rhemes to the right of nonrhemes, and LINEAR ORDER II arranges sequences of either rhemes or nonrhemes in an ascending hierarchical order. TOPIC PLACEMENT places a topic in initial position and leaves a pronominal copy in its original place.

These rules generate sentences in their normal, unmarked, order. Marked, or emphatic, order is obtained by the application of THEME POSTPOSING, a rule which places non-rhematic material to the right of rhematic material.

SENTENTIAL STRESS ASSIGNMENT assigns the feature [+stress] to any rheme which is not followed directly by another rheme.

In addition to these rules, which assign linear order on the basis of rhematic structure, I have suggested some special rules to deal with sentences including 'complex' constituents, since these are linearized independently of their rhematic status.

A particularly interesting aspect of the interrelationship between sentences which are assigned a linear order on the basis of the complexity of their constituents and other sentences is the fact that the former show an optional THEMATIC COMPLEX CONSTITUENT PREPOSING rule which is practically the mirror image of the more general THEME POSTPOSING. By the use of accepted conventions in transformational grammar, these two rules are reduced to one rule of THEME DISPLACEMENT, and a significant generalization is thus captured.

Several surface structure constraints are proposed to deal with differences in acceptability between sentences with atypical rheme selection.

The relationship between the rules proposed here and the traditional categories of subject and object is also examined here. Whereas the category of object is shown to be dispensable, the category of subject is redefined as resulting from the assignment of a feature, which allows rules lie AGREEMENT to identify one argument without recourse to counterintuitive 'configurational' criteria. This redefinition is shown to be more adequate than the configurational alternative vis-à-vis some apparent irregularities in the application of AGREEMENT.

Finally, the rules proposed here are shown to shed some light on the debated question of the proper analysis of sentences with indeterminate 'subjects'. It is demonstrated that an adequate account of such sentences must take into account factors like rhematic structure, topicalization and genericity.

Although this study deals primarily with Spanish, the principles presented in it must surely be applicable to other languages, especially those with relatively 'free' word order.

Appendix

THE RULES

This appendix contains all the rules discussed in the text. With the exception of the rules which produce emphatic order, only final versions are presented here.

(5.1) RHEME ASSIGNMENT (OBLIGATORY)

$$\left\{ \begin{array}{cc} [+\text{rheme}], & X \\ 1 & 2 \end{array} \right\} \rightarrow$$
$$\emptyset \qquad \begin{bmatrix} 2 \\ 1 \end{bmatrix}$$

Condition: X is any element in semantic structure.

(6.2) If the predicate has the feature [+passive], the patient interchanges rank with the agent, cause, possessor or experiencer.

(6.16) The predicate always ranks one step higher than the lowest ranking argument, except when the predicate is [+presentational], in which case its rank is lower than that of the predicate.

(6.21) If the verb has the feature [+presentational], the patient interchanges its rhematic rank with that of the other argument present.

(7.31) RHEME SELECTION HIERARCHY

1. Instrumental, manner adverbial, 'strong' time and place adverbial

2. Target

3. Complement, source, location, time, identifier, beneficiary

4. Patient

5. Agent, cause, possessor, experiencer

6. 'Weak' time and place adverbial

(8.4) LINEAR ORDER I (OBLIGATORY)

$$\left\{ \begin{array}{cc} X & Y \\ [-\text{rheme}] & [+\text{rheme}] \\ 1 & 2 \end{array} \right\} \rightarrow 1 + 2$$

(8.19) LINEAR ORDER II (OBLIGATORY)

$$\left\{ \begin{array}{cc} X & Y \\ [\alpha\text{rheme}] & [\alpha\text{rheme}] \\ 1 & 2 \end{array} \right\} \rightarrow 1 + 2$$

Condition: 2 ranks higher than 1 in the RSH

(8.24) RHEME SPLITTING (OBLIGATORY)

$$
\begin{array}{ccc}
\text{Predicate} + & X & + \quad Y \\
[-\text{rheme}] & [+\text{rheme}] & [+\text{rheme}] \\
1 & 2 & 3 \quad \rightarrow \\
2 + 1 & \emptyset & 3
\end{array}
$$

(9.6) TOPIC ASSIGNMENT (OPTIONAL)

$$
\begin{array}{cc}
\left\{ [+\text{topic}], & \begin{array}{c} X \\ [-\text{rheme}] \end{array} \right\} \\
1 & 2 \quad \rightarrow \\
\emptyset & \begin{bmatrix} 2 \\ 1 \end{bmatrix}
\end{array}
$$

(9.12) TOPIC PLACEMENT (OBLIGATORY)

$$
\begin{array}{cc}
\begin{bmatrix} X & + & Y \\ & & [+\text{topic}] \end{bmatrix}_S \\
1 & 2 \quad \rightarrow \\
2 \;\#\; 1 & \begin{bmatrix} 2 \\ [+\text{pro}] \end{bmatrix}
\end{array}
$$

(9.28) GENERIC PRONOUN DELETION (OPTIONAL)

$$
\begin{bmatrix} +\text{topic} \\ +\text{pro} \\ +\text{generic} \end{bmatrix}
$$

$$
\begin{array}{c}
1 \quad \rightarrow \\
\emptyset
\end{array}
$$

(10.5) THEME POSTPOSING (OPTIONAL)

$$
\begin{array}{cc}
\begin{array}{c} X \\ [-\text{rheme}] \end{array} + & \begin{array}{c} Y \\ [+\text{rheme}] \end{array} \\
1 & 2 \quad \rightarrow \\
\emptyset & 2 + 1
\end{array}
$$

Conditions:

(10.6) THEME POSTPOSING is applicable only if the sentence is an assertion.

(10.16) If X includes the predicate, it must also include all other elements with the features [-rheme, -topic].

(10.56) THEME POSTPOSING is inapplicable to an element X showing the features [+topic, +generic].

(10.13) POSTPOSED PREDICATE MOVEMENT (OBLIGATORY)

$$
\begin{array}{ccc}
X & + \quad Y & + \quad Z \\
[+\text{rheme}] & [-\text{rheme}] & \begin{array}{c}\text{Predicate}\\ [-\text{rheme}]\end{array} \\
1 & 2 & 3 \quad \rightarrow \\
1 + 3 & 2 & \emptyset
\end{array}
$$

(10.38) The acceptability of a sentence decreases in inverse proportion to the number of violations of the rhematic hierarchy.

(10.39) A surface structure with two adjacent rhemes is less acceptable if they are not contiguous in the RSH than if they are.

(10.45) A surface structure is unacceptable if it contains a non-topicalized patient which violates the rhematic hierarchy.

(10.52) A surface structure containing a post-rhematic topic is more acceptable if the topic is in final position than if it is not.

(11.9) SENTENTIAL STRESS ASSIGNMENT (OBLIGATORY)

$$X \quad + \quad \underset{[+rheme]}{Y} \quad + \left\{ \left[\begin{matrix} Z \\ [-rheme] \\ \# \end{matrix} \right] \right\}$$

$$1 \qquad\qquad 2 \qquad\qquad 3 \quad \rightarrow$$

$$1 \qquad \left[\begin{matrix} 2 \\ [+stress] \end{matrix} \right] \qquad 3$$

where # indicates a sentence boundary, and Z is one constituent

(12.19) COMPLEX CONSTITUENT POSTPOSING (OBLIGATORY)

$$[X]_S \quad + \quad Y$$

$$1 \qquad\qquad 2 \quad \rightarrow$$

$$\emptyset \qquad\qquad 2 + 1$$

(12.37) COMPLEX CONSTITUENT PREPOSING (OPTIONAL)

$$X \quad + \left[\begin{matrix} Y \\ [-rheme] \end{matrix} \right]_S$$

$$1 \qquad\qquad 2 \quad \rightarrow$$

$$2 + 1 \qquad\qquad \emptyset$$

Condition: the sentence is an assertion

(12.42) THEME DISPLACEMENT (OPTIONAL) (collapses (10.5) and (12.37))

$$X \quad + \left[\begin{matrix} Y \\ [-rheme] \end{matrix} \right]_{<S>} \quad + \quad Z$$

$$<^*> 1 \qquad\qquad 2 \qquad\qquad 3 \quad \rightarrow$$

$$1 \qquad\qquad \emptyset \qquad\qquad 3 + 2$$

Conditions:
a) the sentence is an assertion (=10.6);

b) if Y includes the predicate, it must also include all other elements with the features [-rheme, -topic]

c) the rule does not apply to an element Y with the features [+topic, +generic] (=10.56).

(12.59) RHEMATIZER POSTPOSING (OPTIONAL)

$$X \quad + \quad Y \quad + \quad Z$$
$$[+rheme]$$

1	2	3	→
Ø	2 + 1	3	

Condition: X is a rhematizer

(12.62) RHEMATIZER PREPOSING (OPTIONAL)

$$\text{Predicate} + \quad X \quad + \quad Y$$
$$[-rheme] \qquad\qquad\qquad [+rheme]$$

1	2	3	→
2 + 1	Ø	3	

Condition: X is a rhematizer

(13.24) SUBJECT SELECTION (OBLIGATORY)

Assign the feature [+subject],

a) in a structure with a patient and an identifier,

 (i) if one argument is [+third person] and the other
     [-third person], to the latter;
 (ii) if they differ in number, to the argument marked
     [+plural];

b) in other structures, to the highest ranking argument in
   the following hierarchy: agent, instrument, experiencer,
   patient, identifier.

(13.25) The verb agrees in person and number with the argument having
   the feature [+subject].

(14.11) The subject-selection hierarchy may be optionally altered
   when the highest ranking argument is indeterminate.

REFERENCES

The starred items are sources of data.

*Alvarez Quintero
    1910   Comedias escogidas. Madrid.

*Arguedas, José María
    1973   Todas las sangres. Lima: Peisa.

*Arniches y Barrera, Carlos
    1948   Teatro completo, vol. 1. Madrid.

*Azuela, Mariano
    1939   Los de abajo. F.S. Crofts and Co.

 Bach, Emmon
    1970   'Problominalization.' Linguistic Inquiry 1.121-2.

    1975   'Order in base structure.' In Charles N. Li (ed.),
              Word Order and Word Order Change. University of Texas
              Press.

*Baroja, Pío
    1918   Mala hierba. Madrid.

 Bello, Andrés
    1847   Gramática de la lengua castellana destinada al uso de
              los americanos. Santiago de Chile.

*Benavente, Jacinto
    1923   Los malhechores del bien. Macmillan.

 Bolinger, Dwight
    1952   'Linear modification.' PMLA 67.1117-44.

    1954   'English prosodic stress and Spanish sentence order.'
              Hispania 37.152-6.

    1954-5 'Meaningful word order in Spanish.' Boletín de Filolo-
              gía, Universidad de Chile 7.45-56.

 Bresnan, Joan
    1970   'An argument against pronominalization.' Linguistic
              Inquiry 1.122-3.

*Cela, Camilo José
    1951   La colmena. Buenos Aires.

    1952   Del Miño al Bidasoa. Barcelona.

 Chafe, Wallace
    1970   Meaning and the Structure of Language. University of
              Chicago Press.

    1974   'Language and consciousness.' Language 50.111-33.

 Chomsky, Noam
    1957   Syntactic Structures. Mouton.

    1965   Aspects of the Theory of Syntax. MIT Press.

    1969   'Deep structure, surface structure and semantic inter-
              pretation.' Indiana University Linguistics Club.

    1970   'Some empirical issues in the theory of transformational grammar.' Indiana University Linguistics Club.

*Clarasó, Noel
    1953   Pigmalion 1950. Barcelona.

Contreras, Heles
    1974   'Indeterminate-subject sentences in Spanish.' Indiana
            University Linguistics Club.

Curry, H.B.
    1961   'Some logical aspects of grammatical structure.' In
            Roman Jakobson (ed.), Structure of Language and its
            Mathematical Aspects, Proceedings of the Twelfth Sym-
            posium in Applied Mathematics, pp. 56-68. Providence,
            R.I.: American Mathematical Society.

Daneš, František
    1967   'Order of elements and sentence intonation.' In To Hon-
            or Roman Jakobson, pp. 499-512. Mouton.

*Díaz Cañabate, Antonio
    1952   Historia de una tertulia. Valencia.

Dougherty, Ray
    1969   'An interpretive theory of pronominal reference.'
            Foundations of Language 5.488-519.

Dubský, J.
    1960   'L'inversion en espagnol.' Sborník Prací Filosofické
            Fakulty Brněnské University A8.111-22.

Emonds, Joseph
    1969   Root and Structure-Preserving Transformations. Indiana
            University Linguistics Club.

Fillmore, Charles
    1968   'The case for case.' In E, Bach and R.T. Harms (eds.),
            Universals in Linguistic Theory. Holt, Rinehart and
            Winston.

    1971   'Some problems for case grammar.' Working Papers in
            Linguistics No. 10, Ohio State University.

Firbas, Jan
    1964   'On defining the theme in functional sentence analysis.'
            Philologica Praguensia 8.170-6.

    1966   'Non-thematic subjects in contemporary English.' Tra-
            vaux Linguistiques de Prague 2.239-56.

Fontanella, Beatriz
    1966   'Comparación de dos entonaciones regionales argentinas.'
            Thesaurus 21.3-15.

Francis, Nelson
    1966   Review of Brno Studies in English vol. 4, in Language
            42.142-9.

Gili y Gaya, Samuel
    1961   Curso superior de sintaxis española. 8th edition.
            Barcelona.

Goldin, Mark
    1968   Spanish Case and Function. Georgetown University Press.

Greenberg, Joseph
        1963   'Some universals of grammar with particular reference
                to the order of meaningful elements.' In J. Greenberg,
                (ed.) Universals of Language, pp. 58-90. Cambridge,
                Mass.

Grinder, John, and P.M. Postal
        1971   'Missing antecedents.' Linguistic Inquiry 2.269-312.

Hadlich, Roger
        1971   A Transformational Grammar of Spanish. Prentice-Hall.

Halliday, M.A.K.
        1967-8 'Notes on transitivity and theme in English.' Journal
                of Linguistics, vols. 3 and 4.

Hankamer, Jorge
        1973   'Unacceptable ambiguity.' Linguistic Inquiry 4.17-68.

*Hartzenbusch, Juan Eugenio
        1911   La coja y el encogido. Henry Holt and Co.

Hatcher, Anna Granville
        1956   Theme and Underlying Question. Two Studies of Spanish
                Word Order. Word vol. 12, supplement No. 3.

Hockett, Charles
        1958   A Course in Modern Linguistics. Macmillan.
                Spanish version by Emma Gregores and Jorge Suárez,
                Buenos Aires: Eudeba.

Hooper, Joan
        1973   'On assertive predicates.' UCLA Papers in Syntax No. 5.

        _____ and Tracy Terrell
        1974   'A semantically based analysis of mood in Spanish.'
                Hispania 57.

        _____ and Sandra Thompson
        1973   'On the applicability of root transformations.'
                Linguistic Inquiry 4.465-97.

Hope, Edward
        1973   'Non-syntactic constraints on Lisu noun phrase order.'
                Foundations of Language 10.79-109.

Huckin, Thomas
        1973   'The variable-deletion hypothesis.' Unpublished paper,
                Seattle, Washington.

Jackendoff, Ray
        1971   'Gapping and related rules.' Linguistic Inquiry 2.21-
                36.

        _____
        1972   Semantic Interpretation in Generative Grammar. MIT
                Press.

Kahane, Henry, and Renée Kahane
        1950   'The position of the actor expression in colloquial
                Mexican Spanish.' Language 26.236-63.

Kayne, Richard
        1971   'A pronominalization paradox in French.' Linguistic

                    Inquiry 2.237-41.

Kiefer, Ferenc
        1967   On Emphasis and Word Order in Hungarian. Mouton.

Koutsoudas, Andreas
        1970   'Gapping, conjunction reduction, and coordinate delet-
                ion.' Indiana University Linguistics Club.

Lakoff, George
        1965   On the Nature of Syntactic Irregularity. Indiana Uni-
                versity Ph.D. dissertation.

        _____ 1968   'Pronouns and reference.' Indiana University Linguis-
                tics Club.

        _____ 1969   'On generative semantics.' Indiana University Linguis-
                tics Club.

Lancelot et al.
        1660   Grammaire générale et raisonnée.

Langacker, Ronald
        1968   'Mirror image rules in natural languages.' Mimeo.
                University of California, San Diego.

        _____ 1969   'On pronominalization and the chain of command.' In
                D. Reibel and S. Schane (eds.), Modern Studies in Engl-
                ish. Prentice-Hall.

        _____ 1974   'Movement rules in functional perspective.' Language
                50.629-64.

Lees, Robert, and E.S. Klima
        1963   'Rules for English pronominalization.' In D. Reibel
                and S. Schane (eds.), Modern Studies in English. Pren-
                tice-Hall.

Lenz, Rodolfo
        1944   La oración y sus partes. Santiago de Chile.

*Martínez Sierra, G.
        1926   Sueño de una noche de agosto. Henry Holt and Co.

Mathesius, Vilém
        1928   'On linguistic characterology with illustrations from
                modern English.' In J. Vachek (ed.), A Prague School
                Reader in Linguistics, Indiana University Press, 1964.

McWilliams, Ralph Dale
        1954   'The adverb in colloquial Spanish.' In H.R. Kahane and
                A. Pietrangeli (eds.), Descriptive Studies in Spanish
                Grammar. University of Illinois Press.

*Medio, Dolores
        1953   Nosotros los Rivero. Barcelona.

*Miró, Gabriel
        1947   Las cerezas del cementerio. Madrid.

*Naranjo, Carmen
        1974   Los perros no ladraron. San José, Costa Rica.

Navarro Tomás, Tomás
      1944   Manual de entonación española. Hispanic Institute, New York.

Otero, Carlos
      1972   'Acceptable ungrammatical sentences in Spanish.' Linguistic Inquiry 3.233-42.

*Palacio Valdés, Armando
      1933   Sinfonía pastoral. American Book Co.

*Pérez Galdós, Benito
      1924   La loca de la casa. Henry Holt and Co.

Perlmutter, David
      1971   Deep and Surface Structure Constraints. Holt, Rinehart and Winston.

Real Academia Española
      1925   Gramática de la lengua española. 15th edition. Madrid.

————— 1973   Esbozo de una nueva gramática de la lengua española. Madrid.

Ringo, Elbert W.
      1954   'The position of the noun modifier in colloquial Spanish.' In H.R. Kahane and A. Pietrangeli (eds.), Descriptive Studies in Spanish Grammar. University of Illinois Press.

Rivero, María Luisa
      1971   'Mood and presupposition in Spanish.' Foundations of Language.

Ross, John
      1967a   'Gapping and the order of constituents.' Unpublished paper.

————— 1967b   'On the cyclic nature of English pronominalization.' In To Honor Roman Jakobson, Mouton. Also reproduced in D. Reibel and S. Schane (eds.), Modern Studies in English. Prentice-Hall.

————— 1967c   Constraints on Variables in Syntax. MIT Ph.D. dissertation.

*Rulfo, Juan
      1955   Pedro Páramo. Mexico.

*Sains de Robles
      1952   Teatro español: 1950-1. Madrid.

Sanders, Gerald
      1969   'Invariant ordering.' Indiana University Linguistics Club.

Shaumjan, S.K., and Soboleva
      1963   Applikativnaja poroždajuščaja model' i isčislenic transformacij v russkom jazyke. Moscow: Izdatel'stvo Akademii Nank SSSR.

148   Heles Contreras

Silva-Fuenzalida, Ismael
        1952-3   'Estudio fonológico del español de Chile.' Boletín de
                 Filología, Universidad de Chile.

Staal, J.F.
        1967   Word Order in Sanskrit and Universal Grammar. Foundat-
                 ions of Language Supplementary Series No. 5.

Stiehm, Bruce
        1975   'Spanish word order in non-sentence constructions.'
                 Language 51.49-88.

Stockwell, R.P., and J.D. Bowen
        1965   The Phonological Structures of English and Spanish.
                 University of Chicago Press.

Terrell, Tracy
        Forthcoming 'Assertion and presupposition in Spanish comple-
                     ments.' To appear in the Proceedings of the Texas Sym-
                     posium on Romance Linguistics.

*Unamuno, Miguel de
        1921   La tía Tula. Madrid.

*Vargas Llosa, Mario
        1966   La casa verde. Barcelona.

*Villarta, Angela
        1953   Mi vida en el manicomio. Madrid.

AUTHOR INDEX

Bach, 16, 19
Bello, 23
Bolinger, 1, 18, 19, 25
Bowen, 105
Bresnan, 16

Chafe, 6, 15, 18, 39
Chomsky, 4, 5, 8, 9, 19-22,
    25, 85, 124
Contreras, 137
Curry, 19

Daneš, 16, 17, 18
Dougherty, 16
Dubský, 18, 25

Emonds, 14

Fillmore, 39, 124, 126, 130
Firbas, 6, 16-18
Fontanella, 105
Francis, 18

Gili y Gaya, 16, 22-24
Goldin, 129
Greenberg, 17
Gregores, 105
Grinder, 16

Hadlich, 25
Halliday, 5, 39, 40
Hankamer, 10, 11, 16
Hatcher, 25, 55, 56, 87
Hockett, 105
Hooper, 12, 14-16
Hope, 21
Huckin, 16

Jackendoff, 4, 11, 16

Kahane, 24
Kayne, 16
Kiefer, 19
Klima, 16
Koutsoudas, 16

Lakoff, 5, 6, 16, 20, 129
Lancelot, 25
Langacker, 16, 62, 115
Lees, 16
Lenz, 23

Mathesius, 16-18
McWilliams, 24

Navarro, 105

Otero, 131

Perlmutter, 42, 95
Postal, 16

Ringo, 24
Rivero, 16
Ross, 16, 95

Sanders, 19
Saussure, 17
Shaumjan, 19
Silva-Fuenzalida, 105
Soboleva, 19
Staal, 19
Stiehm, 1, 25
Stockwell, 105
Suárez, 105

Terrell, 14, 16
Thompson, 12, 14, 15